Tales from the Forgotten Front

Tales From The Forgotten Front

British West Africa during World War II

John Wade

Whittles Publishing

Published by
Whittles Publishing Ltd.,
Dunbeath,
Caithness, KW6 6EG,
Scotland, UK
www.whittlespublishing.com

ISBN 978-184995-126-5

Print managed by Jellyfish Solutions Ltd

Contents

British West Africa, as it was at the time British soldiers were sent
there in 1943 – from a World War II government pamphlet.

Introduction

My father, surely the most reluctant soldier ever to be conscripted into the British Army, once told me that he was the sole survivor of his regiment. It was Anton Walbrook, he assured me, who had saved his life.

Growing up in the 1950s, not long after the end of World War II, I had no idea what he was talking about. Later, I discovered Anton Walbrook was an Austrian-born actor, who emigrated to Hollywood where he played the part of a composer in the 1941 film *Dangerous Moonlight*. An integral part of the plot was a piece of music called the *Warsaw Concerto* which became incredibly popular at the time. My dad was an amateur, but nevertheless proficient, pianist who could knock off this quasi-classical piece at a moment's notice.

'So there we were, lined up on the quayside, waiting to board a troop ship bound for Burma,' said Dad. 'Down comes the colonel, to shake all our hands and tell us what a brave bunch we all are and you could see in his eyes that he never expected us to come back.

'He gets to me and he looks under my tin hat and he says, "You're that man Wade aren't you?" I say yes I am. He says, "The soldier who plays the *Warsaw Concerto* every night in the NAAFI [Navy, Army and Air Force Institutes]?" I nod, and say "yes sir" and he says, "The men enjoy that. We can't have you buzzing off to Burma. We need a pianist in the NAAFI to help keep the men's morale up." And he sends me back to the barracks. Three miles outside the harbour, the ship was torpedoed and went down with all hands. That's how I came to be the sole survivor of my regiment,' said Dad. 'All thanks to Anton Walbrook.'

Whether or not that story was true, I never found out. Like many of my dad's stories, I suspect that it might have been embellished a bit, or even a lot. Because although he had spent two years of his life in Africa during World War II – and was among the lucky ones who didn't get shipped off to fight in Burma – he refused to speak about his experiences, other than the sometimes unexpected humour of his life there and the strange environment in which he found himself as a young man in his late twenties.

There was the story about the day he asked one of the Africans to fill a kettle. After nearly an hour had passed with no sign of man or kettle, Dad went to investigate and found the man beside a stream, using a spoon to fill the kettle through the spout. Dad used to laugh a lot at that one.

As far as I was concerned, then, my dad's war consisted of going to this tropical paradise, full of funny natives and playing the piano in the NAAFI. If you tried to build up a picture of what his life was really like in Africa, you could be forgiven for thinking that the worst thing that happened to him was when he contracted an infection that resulted in the soles of his feet itching so badly he had had to scratch them with a fork until they bled.

As I grew up, in those post-war years, part of a generation that had never actually been touched by war, I sometimes found myself wondering what my dad, not to mention the British Army in general, were doing in West Africa. I was too young and wasn't curious enough to ask in those days, and of course after Dad died it was too late to find the answers. But then I discovered the scrapbooks and diaries he had compiled during his two-year stint between 1943 and 1945, and I vaguely remembered him saying, 'Being in a place like that could drive you mad if you didn't have something to occupy your mind. Some of the blokes

One of the scrapbooks that began a quest to find out more about my father's time in Africa during World War II.

took up needlework or knitting. I kept scrapbooks. The alternative was to start drinking the palm wine, and that way lay madness.'

Among the things that my dad had stuck in his scrapbooks were a series of watercolour paintings and pencil drawings he had completed overseas. Together with these were other drawings made by his army mates, notes he had made about his experiences, bits of poetry written by friends, a whole heap of postcards of the area where he was stationed, other amateur photographs, crudely produced newsletters about people in the regiment, letters to and from home he had written and received, plus documents and government pamphlets issued to the soldiers.

The diaries and scrapbooks made me investigate further, but I discovered that this seemed to be a largely forgotten front, rarely mentioned by war historians. Further research brought some information about what the British Army was doing in Africa at that time. But the big picture of the war was not nearly as interesting to me as the small picture detailed in my dad's diaries, the pictures and pamphlets, his scribbling and his admittedly amateurish watercolour paintings and drawings. To this fascinating information, I added other facts and feelings gleaned from letters my father had written to his parents, to my mother and to her parents. They had been kept safely by my mother for more than seventy years and revealed, when I was eventually privileged to read them, a never before glimpsed, unexpectedly romantic, even poetic, side of my father.

Gradually, with the help of all this data, I pieced together a very personal account of what life must have been like day to day on this forgotten front, a region of the world known as the White Man's Grave, for soldiers like my father, Corporal Sidney Wade, army number 7647523.

The Reluctant Soldier

Sid Wade wasn't really cut out for the army. He used to say that countless sergeant majors had shouted at him and said they'd never make a soldier out of him, and under his breath he would mutter, 'No, I'll see that you don't.' Born in Barking, part of Essex then, and now a Greater London Borough, he left school at 14, with his mind set on being a motor mechanic. His father saw no future in that and convinced him that he would be better off serving an apprenticeship as a printer in the company where he himself worked. So reluctantly, as a young man, scarcely more than a boy, Sid went to work at De La Rue, a prestigious printer of stamps, playing cards and Japanese bank notes. One of his first jobs was cleaning up at the end of every day, sweeping up and burning all the stamps that had been misprinted – the kind of thing for which collectors today pay a fortune.

Printing was a profession he was to pursue for the rest of his working life, eventually running his own business, before retiring to run a sweet shop on the Essex coast.

But back in his early, pre-army years his life away from work was one of continual self-improvement. In his spare time he became an avid reader of everything from history books to the novels of Charles Dickens, which he knew inside out. He developed a wide-ranging general knowledge and studied classical piano to a level only just short of concert pianist standard. He painted in watercolours and oils, played cricket and tennis, and met his future wife at the local tennis club.

Into the army

As Sid grew up, he became a conscientious objector, but peer pressure and the shame it could bring to families in those days made him relinquish his principles. In 1940 he was conscripted into the British Army and issued with his Pay Book, which would accompany him throughout his army career. It described him as 5ft 8½ inches tall, weight 133 lbs, chest 34½ inches, complexion pale, eyes grey, hair dark brown. He was stationed at

Portsmouth in the Fourth Training Battalion Royal Army Ordnance Corps (RAOC). Life was not as bad as he had anticipated as a letter, written to home soon after his arrival, indicated:

18th October 1940

I have at last been issued with a number and all that goes to make a soldier. I have a uniform all complete, and the wonder is, it fits quite well. Except for little pangs of home sickness which hurt a lot while they last, I am fairly contented so far.

We were taken out for drill this morning and I found this quite interesting. After which we were given a lecture by the Commanding Officer. The food remains quite good and, taking it on the whole, everything is quite good.

The hurt comes when the evenings come round. Although I find the reading room comfortable and nice, I can't help thinking of home and I have not yet mastered that lump in the throat which rises at the thought. I began to pack my civilian clothes today, but turned it in until tomorrow. I just had not the heart to do it.

One lucky fellow has just been drafted to London. When he came round to shake hands with us all, he told us that he was glad to go to London as he was an organist, and he told me of all the London organs he has played. You can guess how much I envied him, both for the organ and his being drafted to London.

One thing I do appreciate in this place is the peaceful nights. The siren goes at nine to nine-thirty, but nothing is heard until the all clear sounds in the morning. Last night, after I had made my bed, I got in at 10 o'clock and the next thing I knew it was time to get up, in spite of very rough blankets and no pillow.

We had one raid during the day but this, like night raids, was a very quiet affair. No one seems to take any notice of them. In fact no one even mentions the war in any way. It seems years since I saw a newspaper or heard the word Hitler.

We have been issued with our trades and I am to be a store man, and if all store men in the RAOC are like my colleagues here I shall like it a lot. If you were to hear the conversations in the barrack room you would think you had come to a public school dormitory. Everyone is of the matriculation standard except me, but this makes no difference, as there is no class distinction among the men by order.

I must close now as I have to walk across the barrack room to get my stamps. However, the post does not go until tomorrow, so you would not get my letter any quicker...

Left: Record of employment as an army tradesman – from Sid's Pay Book.
Sid Wade, reluctant soldier, before his mobilization to West Africa.

The RAOC's responsibilities included weapons, armoured vehicles and military equipment, ammunition, clothing and other minor functions. By now a remarkably erudite young man, mild-mannered and with no real interest in soldiering other than that which the army forced on him, the lowly position suited Sid well. He enjoyed telling a story of the day a curtain pole fell off a window and landed in a pile of equipment in the stores. He reckoned it was later packed up and sent out to someone who had requested, and was expecting delivery of, the rear axle of a military vehicle.

Soon, he was transferred to a new posting in Nottinghamshire and took with him the girl who would soon be his wife. She stayed in lodgings close to his barracks and they met whenever they could, their only private moments being their walks around town or over pots of tea in local teashops. On New Year's Eve that year he wrote to his fiancée's parents:

31st December 1940

It almost seems ironic that this letter should be written on the eve of yet another year of war. We cannot but wonder what the New 1941 will produce and whether, true to anticipation, we will see the dawn of the day of peace.

We also look back over the past year with all its grim and tragic applications, and yet further back, although it may seem we can still remember some happy times even in this eve of turmoil that was known as 1940…

After spending time reassuring his future in-laws that their daughter's happiness was of the utmost concern to him, and that he would send her home again if he felt she was in any way unhappy, he added that he hoped she would stay and that they might even be able find something in the nature of a small home. He concluded:

This is all so different to what we expected, but while we are together I think we can be happy enough, even if our financial question will be one not easily settled…

She stayed and, in January 1941, they were married back in Barking, where they found a house of their own. The war continued, as did Sid's army service, based again in Portsmouth. By 1943, three years a soldier and two years a husband, he seemed to be very much settled into, not to say resigned to, his army life. In the spring of that year, returning to his base after seven days leave, he wrote a letter home, a jumbled mixture of his feelings and circumstances, the war and the fellow soldiers he found himself living with, little knowing what was ahead of him and where he would be before that year was out:

18th May 1943

Dearest.

If only this glorious sunshine had arrived last week. We could have gone into the country, or maybe to Southend and done so much that we had looked forward to doing. I hope that you are taking advantage of it now. If I am fortunate enough to get home on Saturday, perhaps we can go for a walk.

Last night we had three raids over here, but as far as I know, there has been no damage done in this area. In any case, I slept throughout the night and heard nothing. I was a bit worried when I heard that Dagenham [the next town to Sid's home in Barking] had had a heavy raid on Sunday night, knowing that this would mean your experiencing the same raid. I expect that he [Hitler and the enemy in general] will attempt heavy reprisals for the damage we have inflicted by breaching the Ruhr Dam. [This referred to the famous Dambusters raid which took place on 16th May that year, two days before this letter was written.] If this does the damage to his industry that we claim it will, it is a mighty achievement. I hope that he does not select the Power Station [at Barking] to vent his reprisals on. Now that the raids are starting in earnest again, were I you, I should not stay at the Youth Centre while a raid is in progress. A large building like that looks very important from the air.

I don't think the enemy raids can ever again reach the intensity of 1940-41, but these small raids can do a lot of damage before we have had time to prepare. In the old days we knew what to expect and accordingly went to shelter at once, but now we are far more likely to be caught unawares.

I had a medical exam yesterday, which revealed that I am now completely established as A1 and fit for any branch of the forces, in any field. This means that if necessary I can be drafted to any other unit for any duties at any time.

I take a poor view of that, but I have been so fortunate that I must not complain and I may get a few more weekends before anything unpleasant comes along.

I have just been talking to the ex-world champion sculler, J. Barry [British rower Ernest James Barry was five times sculling world champion and later the Royal Barge Master to George VI and Elizabeth II]. He tells me that he could still hold his own in the athletic world if he could only keep off the beer. He tells me that he once missed a £180 prize, more because the night before his race he broke his training rules and had a few pints with some pals. We have been talking about rowing and he maintains that anyone who is willing to keep himself in training and observe rules and tricks of the trade, can be a champion, providing that, between the ages of 16-30 he does not relax and remains a teetotaller. It is strange to hear a lecture on temperance from a man who is a heavy drinker and usually drunk on a Saturday night.

It was in November that year that the fears expressed in Sid's letter about being drafted to any other unit for any duties at any time became reality, as rumours spread around the barracks that he and his fellow soldiers might soon be sent overseas. During two weeks leave, he wrote a letter to his wife, giving it to their lodger and asking her to keep it safe and, should he not be home at Christmas, to hand it to his wife on the morning of Christmas Day. His anticipation proved accurate, and soon after, his unit was mobilized for the start of a long journey into what, for most of the men, was the unknown.

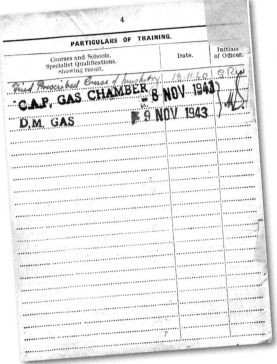

Sid's Pay Book tells the story of his training just prior to leaving England – two sessions in a gas chamber on 8th and 9th November 1943.

The High Seas

Sid Wade was mildly claustrophobic, not enough to affect his life in the way that acute sufferers might not travel on underground trains or refuse to enter lifts, but enough to make him feel uneasy with a need to fight back panic when in crowded places. For that reason, the uncomfortable journey he was about to undertake over the next few weeks must surely have been even more unpleasant for him than for many of his fellow travellers.

It began with a train ride to Liverpool, in which every inch of every carriage and corridor was crammed with soldiers, who were forbidden to leave the train at intermediate stations until it reached its final destination. There, they were transferred to the troop ship that would take them, via a somewhat circuitous route, to Africa. If the train was claustrophobic, it was nothing compared with life on the ship.

Troop ships

Most troop ships, enlisted for carrying military personnel during World War II, were passenger vessels with their fittings stripped back to the bare essentials in order to carry anything up to 10,000 men. In their civilian life, many had been built for speed to keep travelling time to a minimum and so proved their worth in wartime by often outrunning submarines and other enemy craft. Older or smaller ships that were not as fast usually travelled in convoys which offered better protection.

Information on troop ship itineraries in 1943 is scant, but indications from what is available seem to suggest that Sid travelled on the RMS *Orion*. If that was so, it was somewhat ironic that the ship was initially built to showcase a new standard in comfort. Launched in 1934, and first used to transport emigrants to Australia, she was the first British liner to have air conditioning in the public rooms. The modern and ambitious design opened up the ship with removable and folding walls, sliding doors and promenade decks that were enormous, compared with other liners of the day. The extent to which wartime demands resulted in the overcrowding of a vessel like this is best illustrated by comparing the number of passengers she was originally built to take with the number of troops eventually squeezed on board.

As a civilian ship, the *Orion* was designed to take 708 cabin class and 700 tourist class passengers. Pressed into service as a troop ship in 1940, she was converted to accommodate 5,000 military personnel. In 1943, by the time Sid boarded her for his trip to Africa, the troop-carrying capacity had been increased to 7,000.

The 34,000 ton RMS Orion, converted to a troop ship to take soldiers to Africa.

The journey

Transferred from the crowded train to a cold warehouse, then onto the ship, it quickly became apparent that life below decks where the men were to live, eat and sleep for the coming weeks was going to be uncomfortable and claustrophobic. With kitbags and rifles stored in the hold, their few personal possessions were stored in lockers situated above hammocks which were strung from hooks throughout the crowded quarters, relieved only by tables and long benches bolted to the bulkheads, where they would eat. It was two weeks before Christmas.

The *Orion* put to sea, steaming out into the North Atlantic, where it joined a convoy of other troop ships to begin a zig-zagging route south in an effort to avoid enemy submarines. During the day, getting up on deck meant queuing for hours, only to emerge into freezing temperatures and a howling wind. The soldiers realized it was better to remain below decks where long queues also formed for toilets, food and water to wash and shave in. The men quickly became immured to the interminable queues. There was, after all, little else to do.

The North Atlantic has never been known for its calm seas, especially in winter, and the winter of 1943 was no better than could be expected. Within a few days of the start of the voyage, a huge storm blew up. The men were restricted to below decks, as to have climbed on deck would have been to risk being blown or thrown overboard.

Huge waves tossed the ships in the convoy so that, looking out of the portholes, the soldiers saw nearby ships on the crest of a wave high above them at one moment, before plummeting into a deep trough below them the next, as they themselves were carried upwards on the crest of the next wave. As the pitching and tossing of the ships continued relentlessly, seasickness spread throughout the troops, leaving those hardy individuals not hit by it to help their ailing comrades as best they could. Tables and chairs which had been assumed to be safely bolted to bulkheads were torn free and tossed about, along with anything else not lashed down. Most of the men climbed into their violently swinging hammocks, vainly fighting back the urge to vomit and praying for it all to end.

As the convoy continued on its journey south, the storm eventually abated, leaving the quarters below decks in a filthy and wrecked state. Emergency repairs to what passed for furniture were undertaken, floors were mopped free of vomit and gradually life returned again to what passed on a troopship for normal. Queues once again formed for tea, beer, washing water, toilets and the opportunity to grab some air above decks.

Because of the zig-zag course, the ships came close to the coast of America at one point and soldiers who had managed to get on deck crowded the side to catch a glimpse of the American coast. It didn't happen. America remained elusively over the horizon as the ship sailed eastward again, then westward, all the time moving gradually further south. Far from seeing any coastline, all the troops saw was continual sea and sky, until it seemed that any form of land was little more than a distant dream.

Days and nights of sea and sky followed during a voyage that went on for weeks, the soldiers losing all sense of time. Somewhere in the middle of it all, it had been Christmas Day, and 3,000 miles away, a tearful wife was reading a poignant letter that Sid had written back in November. He had left the letter with their lodger, to be handed over should he not be home, or even in the country, for Christmas.

In it, he explained how that year's Christmas wishes were being penned under the most trying circumstances. He wrote nothing of his army life, but spoke nostalgically about their lives together and how much he missed the simple things like their cat and the sound of the railway that backed onto their garden. He suggested that on Christmas Day that year, in his absence, they did their best to both conjure up memories of their previous Christmas together when they had been happier.

He concluded with the words:

> *So, darling, we shall pass our Christmas hours living in the past, yet hoping for the future. The days ahead are obscured in the mystic haze of uncertainty, but for us it is the golden age to be, and I can see us, afar off maybe, but standing firm, bound by a love stronger than earthly bonds. Around us, the glowing rays of hope radiate and reach out, away beyond our sight into the land where "The best is yet to be". God bless you, dear. May He keep us both in loving care and return us safely to each other soon – please, soon.*

It was all a long way from the harsh reality and discomfort of the sea journey Sid was undertaking that Christmas in 1943.

Towards the end of the voyage on the troop ship, the air turned warmer, and then became distinctly hot. The soldiers were allowed to change into tropical clothing. Soon after, land came into sight and, looking through a porthole, knowing little about where he was or what he was doing there, Sid saw a tropical sun blazing down on a harbour full of boats of all shapes and sizes. Between the harbour and distant mountains lay a sprawling colonial-looking town and a church with a square tower that must have looked disconcertingly like any seen in an English country village. The church was actually a cathedral and he was looking at Freetown, the capital city of Sierra Leone.

The 'White Man's Grave'

Sierra Leone's name was derived from one given to it by Portuguese explorer Pedro de Cintra in 1462, who called it Erra Lyoa, meaning lion range or lion mountain. It is said that the name was chosen because of the wild appearance of the land or possibly because of the roaring of thunder around the mountains. It was something that the poet John Milton mentioned in his epic poem *Paradise Lost*, written in 1667, in which he used the words '*black and thunderous clouds from Serraliona*'.

A lion, mountains and thunder contributed to Sierra Leone's name – as illustrated in a government pamphlet.

For centuries, before Europeans arrived in Africa, the region was ruled by powerful and wealthy kings with subordinate chiefs and retainers. Disputes were settled in their own courts of law, not dissimilar to those in what might be thought of as more civilized countries.

The slave trade

Long before Freetown came into existence, the area was strongly connected with slavery. In the 17th century, a harbour located here, formed at the mouth of the Sierra Leone River, was the place where ships called in to pick up consignments of slaves.

When the slaves were taken to North America, they took with them their songs and rhythms, which, many years later, inspired much of American music. As a consequence, spirituals and jazz then developed from the influence of American music on the original African rhythms.

During the latter part of the 18th century, a movement for the abolition of slavery began and, by the 1780s, the number of freed slaves in London had started to grow. The question was, where should they live? British abolitionist Granville Sharp suggested that where would be better than the land from which they came. Accordingly, the British government negotiated with tribal chiefs in Africa to acquire twenty miles of coastline in Sierra Leone and, in 1787, a shipload of freed slaves was brought to the West African coast to build a new life.

Things didn't go well immediately. Around half the settlers died of disease in the first year, some went to work for African slave traders who were still plying their trade, and then in 1789 one of the tribal chiefs burnt the settlement to the ground.

Establishment of Freetown

It was only when it was rebuilt that the settlement was given the name of Freetown and, at last, progress began to be made, as more freed slaves arrived from America, together with settlers from Jamaica. Abolishing the slave trade in 1807, the British government took over responsibility for Sierra Leone the following year. It became Britain's first West African colony, used as a base for a campaign against slave ships.

Because of its reputation for disease, Sierra Leone quickly became known as the White Man's Grave. Nevertheless, over the next fifty years, around 50,000 freed slaves were brought to Freetown by the British. Over the following years of the 19th century, the British began to see the value of enlarging their territories around Freetown, which was fast becoming a valuable port. Towards the end of the century frontiers were agreed with French Guinea and Liberia and, in 1896, Britain declared a protectorate over the region. This angered the tribal chiefs who claimed they had not been consulted, and it led to an uprising in 1898. Subsequently, many of the chiefs were assigned the power of local authority under the main British administration. The only people who chose to venture to West Africa at this time were humanitarians still fighting the slave trade, missionaries spreading Christianity, merchants who traded with the African people and explorers who just went out of curiosity, many of whom never came back.

The British explorer and writer Mary Henrietta Kingsley, who died in 1900, investigated the possibilities of the exploration of Africa, and was given much advice from friends and acquaintances, doctors involved in the research of diseases in the area and literature written by missionaries. Eventually she managed to contact a settler who had lived on the West African coast for several years, and who is reputed to have given her these words of wisdom:

When you have made up your mind to go to West Africa the very best thing you can do is get it unmade again, and go to Scotland instead. If your intelligence is not so strong enough to do so, abstain from exposing yourself to the direct rays of the sun, take four grains of quinine every day for a fortnight before you reach the Rivers [Oil Rivers Protectorate, now known as Nigeria], *and get some introductions to the Wesleyans. They are the only people on the Coast who have got a hearse with feathers.*

In 1900, the West African Frontier Force was formed by the British Colonial Office to garrison the colonies of Nigeria, the Gold Coast, Gambia and Sierra Leone at a time when there were concerns over French colonial expansion on the borders of northern Nigeria. It would become the Royal West African Frontier Force in 1928 when it received royal patronage.

By 1914, a new Empire had been established, which laid down the foundations for modern African states. Involvement in World War I, which broke out that year, was small, apart from the easy and fast surrender of two German colonies – Togoland and Kamerun – to British and French forces in 1914. Being a new part of the empire, there was a recruitment drive by the British among the native population, but few were involved in combat roles.

In the years leading up to the outbreak of World War II in 1939, little changed in the Sierra Leone region. Forts were built and maintained, mainly to protect merchants. Skirmishes and battles were fought between tribes and, on occasions, against British forces who often underestimated the loyalty of the Africans to their own land and their ability for aggression.

As far as disease and its reputation as the White Man's Grave were concerned, however, it remained a fearsome place to live. Any passengers, military or otherwise, on ships that passed through Freetown Harbour en route elsewhere were ordered to stay on board unless they had specific business on land. The chances of catching any of the diseases that were still rampant along the coast were considered not to be worth the risk, however brief the visit.

Before it was discovered that mosquitoes spread malaria and yellow fever, there was a widely held belief that the air itself was bad and the cause of the various infections. The so-called cures for the ailments were often worse than the diseases themselves. They included leeches to suck out the fever from a patient's shaved head, and even treatment with mercury. This was supposed to encourage salivation, but more often had the effect of inflaming the mouth or causing the patient to suffocate on his own swollen tongue.

The effects of war

Because Sierra Leone was part of the British Empire, the colony was automatically pulled into the conflict when Britain declared war on Germany. The Africans were not conscripted, but tribal chiefs were used by the British to encourage enlistment. The colonies were to prove their usefulness to the British war effort, providing troops and labourers for the West African Military Labour Corps, as well as raw materials.

When war broke out in 1939, the total armed forces in the Calabar Province of Southern Nigeria amounted to just 132 African policemen with three European officers to watch over a population of 960,000 people. In addition to the normal maintenance of law and order, traffic regulations and the issue of licences, this tiny force now found themselves responsible for wartime security. With the outbreak of war, Freetown became a strategic base and convoy station for the Allies. The British introduced militarization to the city, and America moved troops into newly built installations. Hundreds of cargo and military vessels manoeuvred in and out of the city's well-protected harbour. At the same time, the Gold Coast became the starting point for the Takoradi air route along which reinforcements flew to the Middle East.

The British West African regiments, already in existence at the outbreak of war, were enlarged with seven new brigades formed in 1940, one of which came from Sierra Leone. Of the others, three came from Nigeria, two from the Gold Coast and one from Gambia. Initially, these became part of the East Africa Divisions and fought in the East African campaign, but in 1943, they were reformed into the 81st and 82nd West Africa Divisions, most of whom fought, and suffered huge losses, in the Burma campaign.

As tens of thousands of men were recruited to work in the docks and on construction sites, the population of Freetown doubled in just two years, while the original city dwellers were co-opted to join British forces in their work. Some did so willingly. Others needed a certain amount of coercion. They organized strikes to gain more wages and better living conditions, they complained of racism, but in the end they also made sacrifices to help with the war effort. It was into this environment that Sid Wade and his fellow soldiers were delivered at the end of 1943, a little over four years into a war that was to last for another two years.

Into Africa

At the time of World War II, British West Africa's four territories – Gambia, the Gold Coast, Nigeria and Sierra Leone – together covered 500,000 square miles, with Nigeria by far the largest. Sierra Leone was a territory of 27,900 square miles and with a population of 1,768,480 people.

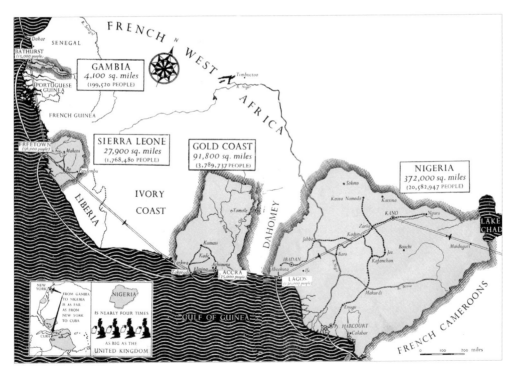

British West Africa, its territories and population at the time of World War II – from a wartime government pamphlet.

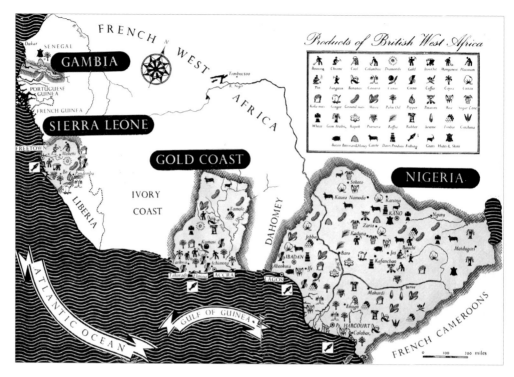

The produce of British West Africa at the time of World War II – from a wartime government pamphlet.

The majority of Freetown's population were Creoles, descendants of those slaves liberated in British territory or rescued by the Royal Navy from slave ships. As a result of the concessions of many years before that had led to local authority being conceded to tribal chiefs, districts and villages in the region were still run on patriarchal lines by dignified old Mohammedans called seyfus and alkalis, overseen by a European Commissioner. By and large, the native chiefs did a good job and many spoke excellent English.

Farmers' co-operative societies were in existence with official encouragement from the British. They were in place to undertake marketing to issue credits to their members. At the outbreak of war, on the Gold Coast alone, there were more than 400 such societies with around 10,000 members.

Much of the daily work was carried out on a co-operative basis. If one man needed help building a house, he would supply food and drink for a large group of people who might get together to help. In turn, he was expected to join another group at another time to offer his help to another neighbour within the co-operative. When work of this type was being undertaken, the host often hired drummers to set the pace and make the work progress better.

First impressions

It was within this completely alien environment and culture, as strange as it was intriguing, that Sid Wade and his fellow soldiers found themselves upon disembarking from their troop ship. There were few white faces to be seen, other than men in uniform, government officials, traders or missionaries. The region attracted very few white settlers.

Marched from the quayside to their barracks, they passed by small compounds where chickens scratching for food were dyed in bright colours to prevent them from straying or being stolen.

Left: Co-operative house builders at work in Sierra Leone.

Above: Freetown landing stage where the soldiers disembarked.

Left: King Street, Freetown – a first look for the newly arrived soldiers.

Freetown tailors weaving native cloth.

Regent Road, Freetown.

The Freetown market.

The streets of Freetown were
full of children.

African traders.

Pounding grain in an outdoor kitchen.

Further on, an open-air market sprawled along the roadside, where long-gowned Africans sold mirrors, cigarettes, tropical fruits, nuts, prayer mats, slippers, leather curios, hippopotamus teeth and home-made soap prepared from wood ash and palm oil. At an open-air kitchen, women pounded grain with long wooden poles, food was cooked over fires in large pots, while a tethered goat looked on.

Colourfully dressed Africans, the women topless, roamed the streets, many with their goods balanced precariously on their heads, all talking and laughing out loud, while over it all hung the pervading smell of dried fish, the local delicacy, and the whirring of scores of sewing machines, operated by jabbering tailors. At the centre of Freetown stood a huge cotton tree that had become a historic symbol of the city. It was said that when the first African American slaves landed there, they walked from the ship to the tree which stood above the bay and held a thanksgiving service to thank God for their deliverance to freedom. It was reckoned that even then the tree was around 200 years old and to this day, it still stands in the centre of Freetown.

The barracks to which the soldiers were headed was on Tower Hill, a name strangely familiar to Sid as that of a London Underground station on the District Line which also ran through his home town of Barking. The barracks, as the name suggested, stood at the top of a hill, a long oblong building with a pitched roof, comprising a ground floor with two floors above. Double doors at the ends of each room opened out, on the first and second floors, onto verandas overlooking the town with the harbour beyond.

Left: Cotton Tree Railway Station, Freetown.

Right: Freetown Docks, with St George's Cathedral in the background.

Top left: Tower Hill barracks.

Bottom left: The view from Tower Hill, over Freetown to the harbour beyond.

Above: African houses were mostly made from mud with straw roofs.

Although the long-term presence of the British meant that many of the Freetown buildings were of traditional brick or wood with slate roofs, most of the native houses around the town were made of mud with straw roofs, a building material used throughout the region, and to astonishing effect at Kano, a walled Moslem city in Northern Nigeria, where arches, domes, buttresses, pillars, parapets and battlements were to be found in the style of a medieval fortress. All were built from conical sun-dried bricks, plastered over with mud.

Freetown's cathedral

Back in Freetown, one building in particular would have seemed to be of a very traditional design to British eyes. Looking for all the world like a typical English village church, it was in fact a cathedral, dating back to the 19th century, when there was a drive to make Sierra Leone a Christian colony.

St George's Anglican Cathedral was built at the instigation of Governor Charles William Maxwell, who ran the colony from 1811 until 1815, and who sought consent for the building from the Secretary of State for the Colonies. The foundation stone was laid in 1817 by Maxwell's successor, Governor Charles MacCarthy and the building took eleven years to complete. The cathedral stood at the head of a diocese that included areas as distant and far apart as Gambia, the Gold Coast, Lagos, Madeira, the Canary Islands, Mauritania and Morocco. It became the venue of worship for major State functions.

From the outside the cathedral, with its typical English church design and tall, square bell and clock tower, must have looked to the soldiers like something out of a village from home, had it not been for the alien African surroundings. Inside, huge stone pillars and arches flanked a nave leading to the altar situated in front of an impressive stained glass window. The congregation were seated in lines of wooden chairs, rather than pews.

Whilst the interior would have seemed extremely British to the soldiers who first saw it, the plaques, busts and inscriptions along the walls told a story that was far more African.

Busts, which commemorated notable people from the region, included: The Reverend William Garnon, first chaplain of Sierra Leone, who began his ministry in the colony in 1816; Thomas Fowell Buxton, politician, philanthropist and slave trade abolitionist, who took over as leader of the abolition movement in 1825; James Africanus Beale Horton, a Creole nationalist writer and British Army medical surgeon from Freetown who had studied medicine in Britain in 1853; and James 'Holy' Johnson, an Anglican bishop in England, who was born in Sierra Leone in 1836.

Left: Looking like an English church transported to Africa, St George's Cathedral, Freetown.

Right: Inside St George's Cathedral.

Inscribed plaques around the walls told their own stories and again emphasized that, although it resembled a British church, the cathedral was truly African. The inscriptions once again reinforced the dangers of living in the region:

> SACRED TO THE MEMORY OF ROBERT CORLEY, RAC CORPS, WHO SURVIVED THE BATTLE OF WATERLOO AND PERISHED IN THIS UNHEALTHY CLIMATE, JUNE 16TH 1837, IN THE 39TH YEAR OF HIS AGE.

> THIS MEMORIAL WAS ERECTED AT THE DESIRE OF THE AFFLICTED PARENTS OF JOHN MANSFIELD, MATE ABOARD HMS THE SCOUT, IN TOKEN OF THEIR UNTIMELY AND IRREPARABLE LOSS FROM THE EFFECTS OF A SEASON SICKLY BEYOND EXAMPLE, IN A CLIMATE PRE-EMINENTLY FATAL TO THE HEALTH AND LIFE OF EUROPEANS. MAY 6TH 1833.

> TO THE MEMORY OF WILLIAM MCCAULEY, HIS MANLINESS AND GENEROSITY, THE TRUE FRIEND OF THE POOR IN THIS COLONY. HE DIED ON 24TH SEPTEMBER 1846, AGED 38 YEARS. THIS STONE WAS ERECTED BY A FRIEND WHO LOVED HIM WELL.

The often surprising mixture of the familiar with the unfamiliar went further than the unexpected existence of St. George's Cathedral. Aside from the Tower Hill name of the soldiers' barracks, there was Waterloo, a city second only to Freetown in size, situated in the west of Sierra Leone; Aberdeen, a neighbourhood on the coast of Freetown; and Hastings, another town in western Sierra Leone.

The currency

There was also something different, while still strangely familiar, about the money that soldiers were about to begin using. At the time of World War II, a little more than thirty years prior to decimalization of money in 1971, the UK operated a three-unit currency system that consisted of twelve pennies to the shilling and twenty shillings to the pound. It was a system that was also used throughout the colonies, and it came originally to British West Africa in the 19th century. At first, because the coinage was the same as that used in Britain, African money was often taken back to the United Kingdom, causing a dearth of coinage in Africa. For this reason, the London authorities set up the West African Currency Board and local coinage, which could not be used in Britain, was issued. The coins were minted by the Kings Norton Metal Company in Birmingham.

Coins in common circulation at the time of World War II had values of one-sixth of a penny, one-tenth of a penny and one penny, with twelve pennies to the shilling. In 1916, two, ten and twenty shilling notes had been issued, followed by a one shilling note in 1918.

An Active Service Army Privilege Envelope, used to send letters home.

A twenty shilling note and four one-tenth penny coins, circulated during the 1940s in British West Africa.

By the time of World War II, however, the lower denominations had been withdrawn and only ten and twenty shilling notes remained in circulation.

Although UK and West African coins had similar values, one big difference in the designs was the inclusion of a hole in the middle. This was to give the Africans a way of carrying their money. Few wore clothes that included pockets, so the coins were designed to be strung on string and carried around the neck.

Correspondence

Communications to home were sent via the Field Post Office, in Active Service Army Privilege Envelopes. The envelopes could contain up to three letters from the same writer, who had to sign to say the contents were purely about private and family affairs and that no valuables were included. The contents were liable to be examined at the army base and each envelope was duly stamped by a censor.

Newspapers

If the troops wanted to catch up on the latest news, there were a surprising number of daily newspapers on offer in West Africa, the majority of which were run exclusively by Africans. Despite an obvious shortage of capital, ten papers appeared every day – four in Nigeria, four on the Gold Coast and two in Sierra Leone. A number of weeklies and bi-weeklies were also published with circulations that could top 10,000 daily.

Left: Bicycle taxi – as illustrated in a government pamphlet.

Right: Wilberforce Street in Freetown, where the bicycle was a popular from of transport.

The coming of the bicycle

Venturing out for the first time, the soldiers found themselves surrounded by throngs of people, all moving at a leisurely pace, as the Africans they were about to work alongside were rarely in a hurry. Not unless, that is, they happened to own a bicycle.

This was a time when the bicycle was beginning to make a serious impression in West Africa and not always in a good way. Many considered that it was becoming so popular that people were losing their skills in head loading, the art of balancing anything they needed to carry on their heads.

A craze was also spreading from nearby Nigeria for taxi-cycles, with seats on the carrier, which might or might not have had a cushion. Passengers sat side-saddle with their legs hanging on one side, ready to leap off if threatened by an approaching lorry. On such occasions the bike rider would 'go for bush', disappearing into the undergrowth with a shrieking passenger and a clatter of crashing bicycle.

Assuming no such accidents occurred, the bike riders charged a penny a mile for a first-class fare. First class meant that the passenger was allowed to remain seated as he or she was pushed up hills. Second-class fares were cheaper, but passengers were required to get off and walk when the going got tough.

It wouldn't have been strange for Sid and his fellow soldiers to see a woman of 15 stone or more sitting sedately on the carrier with a baby bound to her back and an umbrella to protect them both from the sun, while a much smaller and seemingly frail boy pedalled desperately.

Often the bicycles had little or no brakes, which could lead to complications on hills, particularly in spots where a road might dip sharply to a narrow bridge over a stream. Then bicycle rider and passenger would hurtle down the hill hoping to cross the bridge at full speed with sufficient momentum to climb as much as possible of the hill on the other side – and in the hope that there wouldn't be a speeding lorry coming the other way.

It was all a long way removed from the cold, wartime Britain, with its nightly air raids, from which the soldiers had been mobilized only weeks before. In those early days, soaking in their first impressions of this strange land, they must have wondered what they were there to do. They soon found out.

The Daily Routine

During World War II, a number of fronts were well known and have been equally well documented: the Russian Front; the Pacific Front; the Italian Front. However, little was heard of West Africa, it becoming something of a forgotten front during the war. There had been a time when it had been thought necessary to maintain forces in the region due to the possibility of invasion of German forces through Senegal to the north, or from the sea. However, the British and American invasion of North Africa in 1942, otherwise known as Operation Torch, cleared the enemy from the region and decreased the potential risk of a British West African invasion.

Nevertheless, British forces were maintained in the area. One reason was to guard vital supply lines to North Africa, Egypt, India and as far afield as Russia and China. It was well known that the Germans had been looking for ways to exploit the region's resources and labour supply, and the arrival of both British and American forces was instrumental to those plans being put on hold. Freetown also operated as a way station for troops who might find themselves being shipped onto Burma, to fight in one of the longest and bloodiest conflicts of the war, following the Japanese invasion of the country in March 1942. It was a conflict that took the lives of a great many soldiers, who lived under this threat.

In the meantime, the British were also in Sierra Leone to help train African soldiers in the Royal West

The African people were happy to work hard in Freetown docks.

African Frontier Force, many of whom also found their way, along with the British, to Burma. The British found the Africans to be hard workers, willing to load and unload ships, build airfields and roads, improve harbours, drive lorries, work in the fields and on the railways, happy to produce food for themselves and for the troops.

Sid's new life, once the strangeness wore off, and when he could put aside thoughts of being sent to Burma, didn't seem too bad. By now a corporal (the highest rank he would attain in the British Army), and as a member of the service corps, his job was largely to organize and provide necessary supplies to the Eighth Army by rail and air.

Dress code

The soldiers dressed in light tropical shirts, shorts and broad-brimmed bush hats during the day, with the addition of knee-length, suede mosquito boots at night.

Right: Corporal Sid Wade (centre) with fellow soldiers, dressed in tropical gear, photographed in the Freetown studio of the Lisk-Carew brothers.

Below: British soldiers dressed for the tropics – Sid Wade is third from left, centre row.

Added to these, Sid was unique amongst the other members of his regiment in being the proud owner of a thick, woollen balaclava. It had been knitted for him during the winter by his mother and sent to him at his barracks in England, where she knew he must have been feeling the cold. It had arrived just after he was shipped out and finally caught up with him as he sweltered in the tropical heat of Africa.

Climate and disease

The daily battles Sid and his fellow soldiers fought were not against the Germans, but more against the African climate and disease.

From May until the end of October, it was the rainy season. During those months, the heavens opened and rain fell in a solid sheet, lasting most of the day and night. The discomforts of the climate did little to halt the work of the British soldiers who, when not training African soldiers, worked on to: build houses from black rhun palms, whose wood was reputed to be resistant to termites; construct gun emplacements; be drilled in the torrential downpours; and be sent on route marches through the bush.

Occasionally, the sun would break through the clouds for a few brief hours, causing the sodden ground to steam like a Turkish bath. The mangrove swamps would give out a pungent stink of rotting vegetation and clouds of mosquitoes, each one a potential malaria threat, would start to swarm, along with myriads of other biting insects that ranged from ants to sandflies. And then it would start to rain again. Ceaselessly.

When the rainy season ended, the sun would shine diamond bright and blazingly hot, and then would come a hard trade wind called the Harmattan. Dry and dusty, it blew south from the Sahara picking up fine particles from the desert on its way and bringing new misery to anyone unlucky enough to be in its path. By seven in the morning, the day was as hot as the soldiers had known at midday of a hot August at home, then rose to its peak between three and four o'clock in the afternoon.

The Harmattan wind blew and it kept blowing until the rainy season began again.

Disease, as had always been the case in the region, was rife. Apart from the threat of malaria that came nightly from the mosquitoes, the men suffered blackwater fever, caused by heavy parasitization of red blood cells which could lead to, among other nasty things, kidney failure. Yellow fever, an acute viral disease, was equally prevalent, and when you hear that this particular disease was also known as black vomit, you get an idea of its general nastiness. That's without taking into account dhobi itch, a fungal infection causing intense itching and inflammation of the groin, not to mention dysentery, in all its many forms.

Most soldiers were in hospital at least once a month with one or more combinations of these diseases. The alternative – although an unwise one – might have been to seek out the services of the local medicine man.

The African people

Traditionally the African people belonged to tribes. Although some tribes were found throughout West Africa, most confined themselves to specific regions. The largest tribes in Sierra Leone were the Temne, with a population of 550,000, and the Mende, whose population of 1,000,000 spanned both Sierra Leone and Liberia. Other West African tribes at this time, with populations ranging from 400,000 to 13,700,000, included the Akan, Ewe, Fon, Fula, Hausa, Ibibio, Ibo, Kanuri, Mandingo, Mossi, Wolof and Yoruba.

The Africans were a proud race and it showed in their faces.

Historically, the people had been isolated by the circumstances of harsh climate and killer insects. Regular and torrential rain aided the growth of thick jungle with travel between villages being possible only by foot on narrow pathways that were continually overgrown. Mosquitoes killed the people, the tsetse flies killed horses and cattle. The result was a large community of scattered villages, in which farmers struggled to live off the land without horses, cattle or even the most elementary forms of transport.

Because of their isolation, different languages developed among communities who rarely met. In an area perhaps the size of Wales, there might be as many as twenty languages, all distinct from one another.

Then, into this environment came Europeans, willing to teach their ways to the Africans and to offer education, but held back by the problems of dealing with so many languages and reading matter that was only available in English. The Africans were keen to learn history, but how could a teacher explain, for example, The War of the Roses to pupils who had no concept of what a rose might be. If they changed tack and tried to teach African history instead, they were met with suspicion by students who thought that the Europeans were trying to hide their own knowledge. They knew the Europeans were there to govern, and so demanded to know more about European history.

The African people encountered by British forces were pleasant and somewhat shy outside of the towns. They were polite and put great emphasis on their own forms of etiquette, perhaps best illustrated by the fact that there were several different ways of greeting one another, depending on whether the person being greeted was working,

Left: *A fruit seller brings her produce to market.*

Above: *The soldiers found the African people shy but friendly.*

Right: *African farmers and their families toiled in the fields to live.*

walking or in their home. They were very fond of shaking hands, but wary of people who were too familiar with them. The Africans were friendly but expected, in return, respect for their ways of life. They were generous, but expected generosity in return. They had their own codes of right and wrong and their own deeply held religious beliefs. A great many were Moslems, readily identified by wearing long gowns and fezzes, amongst whom polygamy, the custom of having more than one wife, was religiously sanctioned.

In the country, they were farmers who toiled to get enough from the land for families to live on. Men, their women and their children all worked hard in the fields, and it was usually the wives who brought their produce to regular markets, to which people flocked from miles around to bargain for goods. The country folk followed the customs and the religions of their tribes and, although being essentially uneducated formally, they were intelligent, shrewd and wise.

In the towns, the inhabitants were often described as having been detribalized, breaking away from the customs that they had previously adhered to within their tribal societies. They were employed as officials, clerks, labourers, etc., having adopted many of the customs learnt from Europeans and Americans. Some were well educated with degrees from English and American universities, and many had been converted to Christianity. The differences between town and country people had led to the formation of their own class system.

This was the background and the history of the people that the British soldiers now had to befriend. The Africans were naturally suspicious, and trust had to be gained gradually. But when they were able to trust, then they became the friendliest of people.

Much of the Africans' philosophy of life can be gleaned from a small selection of their proverbs:

Boasting at home is not Victory; a parade is not combat;
when battle comes the valiant will be known.

Inquiry saves a man from making mistakes.

Without powder a gun is nothing but a stick.

Things done gently are sure to prosper; things
done by force are sure to cause trouble.

African fables also provided an insight into their thoughts and ancestry. One such fable, told by members of the Akan tribe explained why there were white men and black men:

At the beginning there were two men and their wives who lived somewhere. And the Creator told them where there was a certain fine pool to wash in, and showed them the path to it. And one man and his wife went and washed in the pool and their skins became white.

But the other man and his wife were going to have a meal, and said they would go after they had finished. And when they came to the pool they found that the first man and his wife had used nearly all the water. So they stood in the pool and tried to take up water in their hands. But soon the water was all finished.

That is why the palms and soles of a black man are white.

A tribal fable about black men and white men – as illustrated in a government pamphlet.

35

Medicine men and witch doctors

Not so very long before the arrival of the British, witch doctors still dominated African society. They held their positions by a combination of a genuine skill in herbalism, sleight of hand and the force of their personalities. Although the coming of the white man had compelled witch doctors to abandon some of their more questionable practices, their traditions lived on in the medicine men that were still prevalent at this time.

For a small consideration, the medicine man would mix a potion, make a charm or call upon the gods at times of alarm or disaster, and it was said that their potions were often surprisingly effective. A patient might, for example, be instructed to: '*Take the fin of a fish, the tail of a rat, the head of a snake and the foot of a fowl. Tie together in a bundle, place beneath the nose, inhale deeply, and your headache will disappear*'. The approach might have been different, but the effect wouldn't have been too far away from the result of inhaling smelling salts.

Servant boys

All European troops in West Africa at that time had their own servant boys, who performed simple and often menial tasks for them. Each was fiercely faithful to his master and, it was said, was capable of doing anything, getting anything and knowing everything that was going on, anytime, anywhere. They were looked upon as indispensable and aggravating in almost equal measure, happy to steal, without conscience, from anyone but their master.

Sid's boy was called Sorry Commara and, like all the other boys, he could perform minor miracles for his master. It wasn't unusual for a soldier to trek hundreds of miles into the bush and open his kitbag to find several bottles of whisky in it, 'borrowed' by his boy from some source known only to him.

One soldier told the story of how, when billeted in a small port on meagre rations, his boy managed to regularly feed him extravagantly on superb roast chicken or bush fowl for the sum of two shillings a day. It turned out that he was in league with the cook of a European bank manager who lived next door, to whom he was paying one shilling for plates of food from the neighbour's table.

Servant boy Sorry Commara

The boys knew all the local gossip and often intimate details of the lives of the soldiers they served, and information was veraciously passed around when they all got together to chatter over communal ironing sessions.

Tales were also told of the almost psychic connection they had with their masters. Sailing details in wartime were top secret, and yet it wasn't uncommon for a soldier who had been away overseas for a while to return to Freetown to find his boy waiting for him on the quayside on the very day of his arrival. No one understood how they knew exactly when their master was due to return.

It was from Sorry Commara that Sid learned Pidgin English, the simplified language that develops between two or more groups that do not have a language in common. He soon learnt that for the slow-moving Africans, few things could not be put off until 'the tomorrow past tomorrow' – Pidgin English for saying there was little point in doing today what could be put off until next week.

If something, a small gift perhaps, pleased Sorry, he would explain, 'This is plenty fine, past kerosene, master'. Sid particularly enjoyed telling the story of how he once asked Sorry if he had seen his mate Tommy. The boy went out to look, then came back a few minutes later and said, 'Tommy, him belly walk fine fashion, him legs no agree at all'. What a wonderful description of a drunken man.

In return, Sid taught Sorry, and Sorry taught the other boys, the art of speaking in cockney rhyming slang, something in which Sid was proficient. After that, if any of them were asked the whereabouts of someone who might have gone for a walk down the road, the likely reply would be 'Him go for ball of chalk down frog and toad'. It would be entirely wrong to assume that because the terms 'master' and 'servant boy' were used to describe these Africans and their relationships with the soldiers, that they were treated badly or were uneducated or in any way resentful of their masters. Inevitably there was the odd bad soldier who treated his boy with disdain, but by and large the relationship between the men and their boys was one of mutual respect.

When Sid was due to return home, and to part from his boy for the last time, Sorry Commara presented him with a picture of himself, on the back of which, he had written his master a short note in small, neat handwriting, accurately punctuated and in commendable English:

My Dear Mr Wade.

My contact with some of you British personnels in the Army has really changed my views about British peoples. It has revolutionised my outlook in life, and indeed I have the sincere hope that after this chaos we may surely enter into the new reforms – new life – new freedom – democratically speaking.

I wish you all Agents of the other Country to interpret our needs correctly to the Ministers of various Administrations of Britain, for a better and lasting partnership between Britain, her Allies, the Dominion and the Colonies.

Best of luck, Dear.

Sorry Commara.

Preventing diseases

Disease was always close at hand, and the soldiers were given much advice on how to avoid it.

Malaria, if not treated promptly, was one of the most dangerous diseases for the soldiers, who were ordered to sleep under mosquito nets at all times, tucked firmly into beds and in place before dark. By the time of World War II, it was generally accepted that malaria could be largely suppressed by small doses of Atabrine and quinine. Cold hands, a headache and slight fever were signs that the fever was coming on, but treated promptly it could be little more troublesome than a common cold.

Water was never drunk or used for teeth cleaning unless chlorinated or boiled for at least ten minutes before filtering. Beers and wines, if correctly bottled were considered safe, but milk was always boiled before drinking. Meat and fish had to be thoroughly cooked. The same went for vegetables, after being carefully cleaned. Lettuces and tomatoes were banned.

Soldiers were instructed to keep their feet covered at all times to prevent skin diseases and infection from parasites on floors and rugs. Shoes were to be kept off the floor at night, preferably inside the mosquito net and banged out in the morning to get rid of spiders and scorpions that might have crawled in during the night.

Regular washing and bathing were recommended and iodine was applied to every scratch, however small. Open sores had to be well treated and kept bandaged. Extra salt was taken to prevent symptoms of salt loss through excessive perspiration. Sunbathing, as it had been known at home, was strongly discouraged, and the wearing of sun helmets was mandatory, even in cloudy weather.

The obvious precautions against contracting venereal diseases were also recommended.

African soldiers

The major task of training African soldiers enlisted into the Royal West African Frontier Force was not just to make them ready to fight an enemy that never actually arrived, but more in preparation for their shipping out of Africa and into Burma, where they fought side by side with the British. Boys as young as sixteen joined up in the 1940s, seeing the army as a good job. For most, it wasn't a matter of loyalty to Britain or patriotism. They saw their friends joining up and simply followed, unaware of the troublesome times ahead of them. In fact, more than 100,000 soldiers from the West African Frontier Force were shipped out to Burma.

The African soldiers were drawn from all parts of West Africa, many from fierce fighting tribes of the Gold Coast or Nigeria, most of them making excellent soldiers. They were aware of the fascist regime that was the enemy of their British allies, and therefore now their enemy too, and they were aware of the inherent racism that such a regime engendered. They knew it was in their interests to work with the British and to learn how to fight, and although there were naturally times of dissension, by and large they accepted their new role.

Above: Soldiers of the Royal West African Frontier Force.

Right: Cap badge worn by members of the Royal West African Frontier Force.

British soldiers became very fond of their African counterparts and found that a sense of humour was vital in this work, not least when they discovered the names of some of those under their command. Many of the Africans had been given, or had adopted, names which they thought of as being typically English, and it wasn't unusual to meet someone called Winston Churchill, William Shakespeare or even Oxford English Dictionary. The British soon discovered that if you could make an African soldier laugh it soon got him on your side.

The Africans were very proud of their origins. A typical story was told of the way the Nigerian soldiers were issued with large bush hats, which they wore with pride. Gold Coasters, however, had only forage caps, which the Nigerians laughed and jeered at. When they could take no more of the Nigerians' scorn, the Gold Coasters got together one night, armed themselves with machetes and went out to look for those who had mocked them.

One bloody encounter later, in order to appease the Gold Coasters, they were issued with steel helmets, which they wore with pride, even in temperatures as high as 110 degrees Fahrenheit in the shade. The temperature didn't matter. They had their helmets, they were proud of them and now they had a reason to jeer at the Nigerians – which led to another riot.

The often fascinating and sometimes frustrating aspects of intermingling and interacting with the native population were set out clearly in a government pamphlet issued to the soldiers. It introduced them to: the customs and habits of the Africans with whom they were to work and, when necessary, fight; the things they must do to win the Africans' respect; and equally the things they should never do. It was full of sound advice for any novice to the area, although presented sometimes in a way which, today, we might find somewhat politically incorrect.

An excerpt from the pamphlet is reproduced in the following chapter.

Understanding The African

(From a government pamphlet issued to British soldiers)

A selection of pamphlets
issued to the soldiers.

To understand the African soldier, it is necessary to know something of his background, his customs and his habits. It is said that only two things are true of all the 26,000,000 people in British West Africa. First, their skins are black. Second, the King of England is their 'Father'. For the rest, there is a bewildering complexity of race, tribe, tongue, religion, costume, custom, occupation and outlook.

Some forty chief tribes are listed in the four colonies. In addition, there are many smaller tribes, each with its own dialect. Thus it is impossible to give more than a general – and therefore inadequate – picture of the men with whom the new arrival in West Africa may serve.

It is not so many years since each tribe lived by itself for itself. It warred spasmodically with its neighbours for the possession of women, cattle and crops. Slave trading was a respectable occupation, and human sacrifice a common religious practice in the forest country. Superstition, often in its darkest forms, was rife throughout the West Coast.

All this has changed for the better, but the African still retains many of the superstitions and customs of his forefathers.

The tribal system

One thing that has not changed is the tribal system. The tribe remains as the social unit in each of the four colonies, preserving the best in African communal life, while having enough flexibility to adapt itself, under guidance, to the impact of the new ideas.

The backbone of the tribal system is the peasant farmer – the little man who used to be content to grow enough food to keep himself and his family alive, but who now also grows a cash crop for export. With the cash he gets for his cocoa, his groundnuts, his palm kernels or his rubber, he buys the things he wants from Europe or America. Chiefly it is cotton goods – 250,000,000 square yards were imported before the war – but also high in his esteem are cement for building, kerosene and lamps for lighting, tobacco and cigarettes, hardware, tinned goods and bicycles. In general, however, the tribe supplies his fundamental requirements. The neighbours help him to build his house of mud-bricks or straw, and to thatch the roof. His pottery, stools, mats and coarse cloth, his wooden mortars, pestles and bowels, his rope and his baskets are all home-made. Similarly, the fishing tribes for the most part make their own canoes and nets.

Dancing and drinking

In the fields, his wife or wives do at least as much work as he does himself. The staple crop will be some form of grain, yams, cassava or rice, with side-crops such as bananas, sweet potatoes, beans or other vegetables. His diet is thus largely vegetarian.

Above: *Jig-jigging to the beat of the drum in Sierra Leone.*

Left: *A young African dancer.*

Usually, the African 'owns' the land he works on, in the sense that, although the land is normally regarded as the property of the community, he and his family have gained 'rights' over the piece they cultivate.

He gets most of his fun out of dancing and drumming, without prejudice to an occasional night out on home-brewed palm wine. African dancing is a highly developed art, and the dances are an exciting pattern of movement, rhythm and colour.

It is almost certain that he can neither read nor write. But he shows considerable awareness of the school that has been set up in the village. Even though it means less help on the farm, he insists that his children go to school, if only for a year or two and he is vastly proud of their learning.

Skilled and unskilled

The African is not invariably a farmer or a fisherman. The Fulani people are the herdsmen of West Africa, moving their herds across great tracts of land in search of water and

Freetown fishermen with their nets.

pasturage. The Hausa trader, a strict Mohammedan, is a familiar figure in all the markets of West Africa, usually peddling the wares of Kano.

Kano was a city famous for its craftsmen, but the repute of the goldsmiths and weavers of Ashanti, of the brass-workers of Benin and Calabar, is no less, while the skill of the Timne basket-makers in Sierra Leone has more than local fame. Nearly every tribe has its artists in wood carving.

Besides the skilled there is the unskilled – the man who leaves his tribe for part of the year at least in order to sell his labour to the government or to one of the commercial firms.

This migrant labourer – like the army recruit – poses many difficult problems. The unsophisticated African, suddenly removed from the habits, customs and values of the tribal life and confronted with an entirely different set of values is apt to acquire the vices of the new civilisation in place of the virtues of the old.

The intelligentsia

In coastal towns where the African has long been in contact with the white man, the process of detribalisation is well advanced among some sections of the population.

An intelligentsia has arisen with European habits of life and a European outlook. Not infrequently its members have received the best education that the United Kingdom or America can give. In relation to the mass of the population its numbers are small, but its influence is considerable and it can make its voice heard. Barristers, doctors, ministers of religion, teachers, businessmen, journalists and civil servants are all represented in its ranks.

Already Africans form the major part of the civil service, and they are admitted to high posts as their capacity is proved.

The war has given a tremendous impetus to the training of Africans as technicians. The army is giving training in 65 trades – ranging from topographical draughtsmen, surveyors, dispensers and instrument mechanics to bakers, drivers, sawyers, tailors and welders.

These, then, are the people of West Africa in all their variety…

- The veiled Tuareg arriving at Kano by camel caravan to buy cloth.
- The naked pagan on Jos Plateau.
- The fourth wife winnowing the groundnut crop.
- The woman magistrate with an Oxford degree.
- The aloof Fulani watching his herds.
- The RAF pilot.
- The painted witch doctor.
- The surgeon in the operating theatre.
- The dignified benevolent Emir.
- The patient woman, load on head, baby on back.
- The round-shouldered workers in gold, leather and brass.
- The engine driver leaning from his cab.
- The tribal drummer.
- The radio announcer.
- And the soldier of the Royal West African Frontier Force.

You and the African soldier

Most of the advice offered to the new arrival in West Africa on how to behave towards the African population can be summarised in the sentence: *Behave as you would at home where you are subject to strong local public opinion.*

There is no need to have an expert knowledge of the customs and traditions of the African in order to be able to 'handle him', but the more you know about him the better.

Any new arrival who fails to take an interest in the African and his ways is making difficulties for himself that may have serious consequences when he goes into action, and is lowering the efficiency of his unit.

Meeting the Africans

The African may appear at first a trifle demonstrative, but there is a great deal of sincerity in his showy salutations.

In some parts of West Africa he may call you 'zaki' (Lion), or address you as his 'father and mother', or express the fervent hope that you may live to a ripe old age. These are the outward expressions of a natural courtesy, and need not be taken too literally.

For example, the fact that he calls you 'zaki' does not accord you the status of that beast and give you the power to rant and roar, for if you do you will be deceiving none but yourself.

If you are in a position of authority, then exercise it as you would at home, quietly, firmly and without favour. Endeavour to gain the confidence, respect and trust of those under you. You will achieve nothing by bawling yourself into a frenzy, for you will be spotted at once as one who is not sure of himself, and provoke sullen opposition instead of ready obedience.

Equally, you should avoid too easy fraternisation with the African, for he, like you, is suspicious of those who attempt to make friends among people not of their own colour.

The language difficulty

You should always remember that English is not yet the mother tongue of the African, and that even to one who professes to know English you have to speak slowly, but not necessarily loudly, to be clearly understood.

You will save yourself a lot of annoyance if you appreciate this fact and realise the African's difficulty. This is precisely as great as you would experience if you were compelled to take orders in a language that you do not completely understand.

Though English is the language of the Royal West African Frontier Force and is taught to all soldiers, if you can learn to speak to the African in his own language you will find that your labours have been well rewarded in increasing his confidence and respect towards you.

Though the African's customs and beliefs will appear strange to you at first, it serves no good purpose to laugh and jeer at them. If you remember that your habits and manners are equally strange to him, and observe his acceptance of the differences in your respective modes of life, and try to emulate his tolerance, you will not go very far wrong.

The African dislikes being patronised as much as he resents being treated as a servile inferior. To 'handle' Africans the first essential is that you must be able to handle men; the exercise of this gift is the same the whole world over.

Getting the best out of the African soldier

In the West African Force it is necessary not only to understand the African soldier, but also to get the best out of him under all conditions. The notes that follow have been compiled for the guidance of the new arrival who wants to get at the root of the matter without delay. They are based on the experience of men who have served in the Royal West African Frontier Force for many years.

In the first place, it is important to realise that, in the eyes of the average African soldier – the man who has grown up in a small village, with little or no education – this is 'our' war, and not the Africans' war.

Though he would not like to be on the losing side in a fight, and is not unappreciative of the benefits of living under British rule, he has no clear idea of the issues involved in the war, or of the consequences of defeat.

It is essential, therefore, that each individual European leader of the African soldiers should do all he can to win their respect and whole-hearted support, for, to a large extent, it is to him as their leader rather than to the cause as a whole, that they give their allegiance.

The raw material

The African recruit is a volunteer. His reason for joining up may be pressure from his chief, lack of work, eagerness to learn a trade, or simply a desire to be like the smartly turned out soldiers and bandsmen he sees with a recruiting party.

In a group of recruits in any colony, you may find a small farmer who has been tilling a small piece of land near his village, a herdsman from the north, a hunter from the forest country, or a fisherman – outwardly simple types, with much the same steadfastness of character as the men from the farming districts at home.

Or you may find a labourer who has been employed by a Native Administration or a Public Works Department, or a trader who has been running his own small business and has decided either that it isn't a paying proposition or that there are more pickings and an easier life to be had in the army.

You will also come across the inevitable 'black sheep' who has taken a hint from his chief that it will be to his advantage to get out of the village.

There will also be few who have worked as household servants, and a smattering of schoolboys fresh from a mission or state school who have come to learn a trade.

Lastly, there will be the chosen few who have joined because they genuinely like the idea.

Practically all will be illiterate, and will have to be taught simple English. This is the raw material of the Royal West African Frontier Force. However unpromising they may sound, these men can be turned into smart and well-trained soldiers. There are thousands of them in West Africa today, and many more coming forward. They represent a valuable contribution to the Empire's fighting power. In the technical services they have released many Europeans for service elsewhere.

But they have to be well led, and that is where you – the new arrival in West Africa – come in.

The power of superstition

The average recruit has known only a very simple mode of life. He and his people are bound by ancient customs and laws. Their loyalties are to the head of their family and to the chief. Their tribal responsibilities are mainly financial, but they may also involve such things as attendance at funeral customs, and the observance of festivals. However trivial these things may appear in the eyes of the European, they are of great importance to the African.

The private lives of the Africans are not complex, but they have their social and domestic difficulties as we do, and as any company commander or platoon sergeant will find out for himself when dealing with pay and allotments.

The African is very much influenced by superstition, even the so-called Christian. It is not so very long since the witch doctor-cum-medicine man dominated primitive African

A group of women from Sierra Leone's Bondu Society,
dressed for a ceremonial devil dance.

society. Though the coming of the white man has compelled him to abandon his more questionable practices, such as 'smelling out', his tradition lives in the medicine man. For a consideration the medicine man will still mix a potion, make a charm or propitiate the gods at times of alarm and disaster.

The primitive African uses charms as a protection against every conceivable kind of misfortune. The charm may be a stone reputed to be endowed with supernatural powers, a bird's beak, the skin of a chameleon, the horn of an antelope, the tail of a porcupine, the claw of a lion or a bundle of feathers.

The Mohammedan soldier places his faith in small leather amulets which he wears under his clothing.

Is the African really lazy?

The African's character – like our own – has evolved out of his environment. Time is not of any great importance, and is counted not in hours but by how far one can travel on foot, or how much work can be got through. The sun provides warmth, and the bare necessities of life are usually easily come by.

Judgments and opinions are formed slowly, but the African is shrewd, and when he makes up his mind he usually gets right down to the core of the matter.

His interests are limited, and he has little or no idea of games or sports as we know them – with the exception of association football which is growing in popularity. Instead, he has his own pastimes which are usually played sitting down in the shade.

Hence, by the standards of the more conscientious – and more harassed – European, the African maybe regarded as being rather lazy and slow-thinking.

He can be changed

It is our task in the army, through knowledge of his nature and outlook, to get the best out of him. With training it is surprising how quickly most of his old habits disappear, and there is certainly nothing lazy about Africans trained by competent Europeans.

African troops have a great sense of 'schoolboy honour' which often prevents them from reporting things that ought to be brought to light. Thieving and 'getting away with something' are regarded as clever rather than dishonest.

Though the average African washes himself frequently, sanitation and hygiene as we know them do not exist in his own village. To him the sun is the best disinfectant.

Morals, to our way of thinking, are non-existent among the Africans. Their behaviour is dictated purely by tribal customs and laws, and not by any sense of what is ethically right or wrong. Another man's wife is fair game. Prostitutes, however, are a quite modern invention, and are frowned upon.

The average African is loyal to those with whom he comes into close contact, and he behaves with natural courtesy. Where he has not been spoiled by living in large coastal towns, he has an instinctive respect of position and authority.

The army through African spectacles

That, in brief, is a sketch of the average man who enlists in the Royal West African Frontier Force. Owing to war-time conditions, enlistment nowadays is a completely different thing for him from what it was for the peace-time soldier. Whereas, before the war, the African had his own home and family life while in the army, he is now divorced more or less completely from all he has been brought up to – country, relations, customs, and often his favourite kind of food.

In exchange, what does he get?

First, he is clothed and fed. In many cases neither the clothing nor the food is to his taste.

He is paid on much the same scale as a labourer, which fixes his status in the class-conscious African community. His accommodation is either in tents, huts or barracks which he shares with others; he has no privacy, and that means a lot to the African.

The greatest hardship of all in his eyes, is that he is deprived of his woman, who in private life administers to all his needs, cooks, keeps house and does all the domestic tasks as well as some of the manual ones.

He becomes subject to a new set of laws, customs and rules, many of which are quite alien to his nature. He is also subject to new forms of punishment, which differ from his own.

He has to learn a great many things quickly, is confronted with entirely new domestic and financial problems which he is often unable to solve for himself. He has to learn a new language and serve new and strange 'masters', many of whom know nothing about him.

Inevitably he is subject to the whims of his white superior, whether these be good or bad.

All this does not mean that the balance is entirely against the African soldier, and that he is a disgruntled individual. On the contrary, life in the army has many advantages, and he is usually extremely cheerful.

But it does mean that he can easily become disgruntled if his difficulties and complaints do not receive the consideration they deserve when he lays them before his superior.

Time spent by a European in dealing with African soldiers' queries about pay, complaints about non-payment of allotments, and domestic troubles, is time well spent.

The African in training

How are we to treat the African in training? First, let us consider what we want from him. We want him to learn a kind of fighting that is alien to him, though his grandfather may have fought in a dozen tribal wars.

New methods, new weapons, strange enemies – all these things have got to be explained to him in a way that he understands. He cannot reason things out for himself, and is not mechanically minded. Explanations have to be made to him in a way which, to the average British soldier, would seem childish and a waste of time.

We are, however, dealing with a man who, in these matters, has the mind of a child. Every simple little thing that is self-evident to us must be explained and demonstrated. It is no use saying: 'If you do so-and-so, such and such will happen'. He must be shown the thing actually happening.

He very easily gets into a parrot method of doing things without understanding the reason for them. Stoppages in a light machine gun are a good example. In their correct sequence he will go through them perfectly. But jumble them up, and he is lost. That is one of the dangers of a drill in training for work in the field. A good method of teaching most things is to try to link them up with his own experiences. Many Africans, for example, have hunted game. Compare the enemy to a herd of game which, if it sees or hears you, will make-off. The enemy, on the other hand, will not run away. If you are unwary, he will kill you.

There are endless comparisons, and the African will understand and pick up things ten times quicker by seeing the things we are trying to teach him in relation to things he already knows and understands.

It sometimes happens that this method cannot be used. Gas, for instance, is frightening enough to us, but to the African it is simply 'white man's magic'.

How, he asks, can the air suddenly kill him? The answer is to send him into a gas chamber and let him experience the effects of a gas, either without a respirator or with a badly fitting one. Give him a well-fitting respirator, send him into the chamber again, and let him see the difference for himself. No further explanation will be necessary.

The African on active service

In the East African campaign, it was quite apparent which European had succeeded and which had failed. The troops were only too keen to go into a scrap with the one they knew and trusted. For the one who had failed them before the campaign began, they had no time.

The following are some noticeable points about the African on active service, based on experience in the campaign:-

He will put up with great hardships and discomforts for considerable periods of time without grumbling, if kept cheerful and provided the reason for it all is either apparent or explained to him.

A hot meal puts up his morale at once.

He does not like being pinned down by shell fire or machine-gun fire. African troops must be kept doing something. Whenever possible, try to take them out of a 'sticky' position and do the job in another way. Try to get them forward in small bodies, or anything so long as they are made to do something. If you don't, they will move on their own, and it maybe forward or backward – you cannot tell. If they cannot be moved, it is essential the Europeans go about and talk to them.

The African is not frightened in the same way as we are. His fear is not of being hit, but rather of the unseen weapon, such as the field-gun that is shelling him but cannot be seen.

The West African is not cruel, nor is he easily aroused. But he does not like to see a comrade hit. This makes him very angry, especially when the victim is a European he knows and likes. Once an action is over, they are quite like British troops in the way they fraternise with prisoners. Nevertheless, their idea of war has always been to loot all they can, and they tend to look upon the possessions of prisoners as fair game.

Experience has shown that though the African in action depends to a great extent on his European leader, African non-commissioned officers are capable of taking charge in an emergency and of doing extremely well.

Do's and don'ts

DO learn enough of the language of the Africans under your command to enable you to talk to them.

DO help them to learn English. It is one of your first duties.

DO find out about their country, tribes and customs. They then feel that you are taking an interest in them, and repay you by taking a keener interest in their work.

DO spend time on their problems and difficulties.

DO see they are fed, clothed and housed properly.

DO ensure they understand what is going on, that orders are explained to them and reasons given.

DO ensure they know everything you can tell them about the enemy, his weapons and his methods.

DO see they get their food, etc. after a hard day. The old motto 'Men first, then officers' still holds good.

DO be fair. Be strict, but be fair.

DO treat them like human beings and look after them.

DO make them laugh. It is quite easy to keep them cheerful.

DO remember that by European standards they are children, and that you are their 'father and mother' for the moment.

DO be smart and well turned-out, and they will follow your example.

DO ensure that they get news of their families.

DO help them to keep up their own customs.

DO try to understand them and gain their affection. It will pay handsomely.

DON'T swear at the African soldier.

DON'T shout at him. He just goes dumb and doesn't understand.

DON'T hit or kick him. He doesn't like it, and will get his own back later. Besides, it is a court-martial offence.

DON'T ever be too busy to hear a complaint or to spend time going through evidence. It is time well spent, and you will be repaid for it.

DON'T laugh or jeer at the African's customs and beliefs. He doesn't laugh at yours, which appear equally strange to him.

DON'T interfere with the African solders' women.

DON'T be ashamed of admitting you are wrong.

DON'T lie to them, or try to bluff them.

DON'T be ashamed to ask your troops, if there is something you are not sure about. They will consider it their duty to help you if they can.

DON'T ask them to do something you won't do yourself.

DON'T break your word.

DON'T try to teach them something you are not sure of yourself. Make sure first.

DON'T be mean over money matters.

DON'T expose yourself unnecessarily before the African. This is bad form from his point of view.

DON'T expect too much, too quickly.

DON'T expect confidence, loyalty and respect until you have earned it.

The Wildlife

For a town boy, whose knowledge of wild animals didn't extend much past what he had encountered in London Zoo, the African wildlife that now surrounded Sid Wade and his fellow soldiers was equally strange. Lions, tigers, alligators, hippopotami and the like would have been familiar to him from visits to zoos back home in Britain, but what of some of the more unusual creatures to be found in the region, many of which could easily cause suffering and even death?

Mudskippers

The mudskipper lived in the mangrove swamps that fringed great stretches of the coast. It was actually a fish, but one that spent more time out of water than in it, taking its name from its habit of skipping along the surface of the mud. For legs it used two fins that sprouted from behind its gills. Fully grown it was around nine inches long and extremely ugly, with a large, grotesque, square head crowned by red, bulging eyes.

Manatees

The manatee, in contrast to the mud-skipper, was a land mammal which preferred to live in water. As a result it had acquired a fish-like tail and two fin-like flippers instead of arms. Added to a large, fat body and a head a little like that of a walrus, the man-atee took on a vaguely human-like appearance and is thought to have helped to perpetuate the mermaid legend.

The manatee – as illustrated in a government pamphlet.

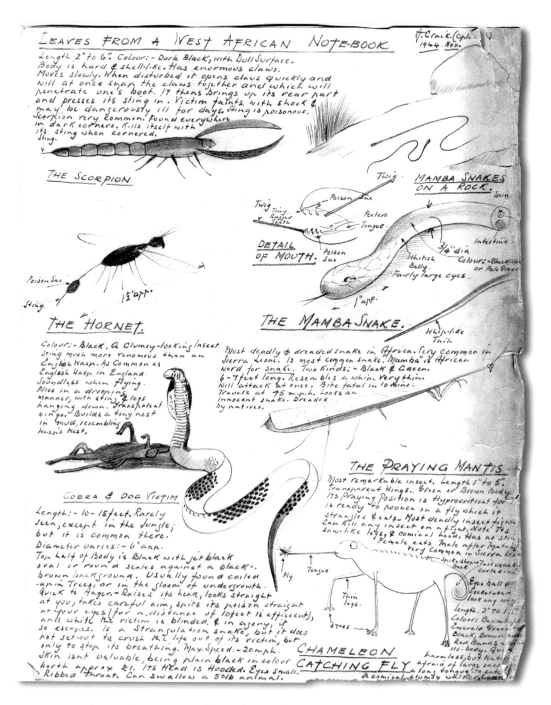

Leaves from a West African Notebook – pencil notes and illustrations of the local wildlife, drawn and notated by an unknown soldier.

Chameleons

No doubt the soldiers had heard of the way some species of these lizard-like creatures could change the colour of their bodies to camouflage themselves against attack by their enemies. But equally curious was the creature's prehensile tail, its eyes that worked independently of one another and a tongue as long as its body. The tongue was used for catching insects, as it lay in waiting, immobile on a branch and blending in with its surroundings.

The chameleon – as illustrated in a government pamphlet.

Snakes

West Africa abounded with a variety of snakes, the three most deadly being the puff adder, black-necked cobra and green mamba.

The puff adder was squat and sluggish, only around three feet long. Its sandy-coloured patterned body blended well with its surroundings, making it dangerous to those who came upon it unexpectedly. The snake was among the most aggressive biters, more likely to attack than to retreat when confronted, and its venom broke down tissue as it spread through the body over the course of twenty-four hours. The cobra, which could grow up to fifteen feet long was rarely seen, except in the jungle, where it was commonly found coiled around trees or hiding in dense undergrowth. Quick to anger if disturbed, it would raise its hooded head, look straight at whatever creature had disturbed it, take aim and spit agonising poison into its victim's eyes. It was deadly efficient up to a distance of around ten feet. Having blinded its victim, it might make its escape, and was capable of speeds of up to twenty miles per hour. Alternatively, it might attack further, strangling its prey by crushing the life out of its victim. It was capable of swallowing an animal weighing anything up to fifty pounds.

Soldiers were warned to beware of snakes – as illustrated in a government pamphlet.

Mamba was the African word for snake, and the species that bore the name could travel at up to forty-five miles per hour. It didn't look particularly dangerous, but was, in fact, known as the most deadly and dreaded snake in Africa, very common in Sierra Leone. Growing up to seven feet long, but very thin, the mamba lived in trees or in the roofs of houses. There were two kinds – black and green – each of which would attack without hesitation, with a bite that could be fatal within ten minutes.

Pythons, up to twenty feet long when fully grown, were also to be found in the region, making their homes in caves or trees. They hunted and fed on creatures as small as lizards and as large as antelopes, and would even attack people when threatened. They killed by coiling themselves around their victims and squeezing. Each time the creature took a breath, the python would squeeze tighter until it had killed its prey, which it then swallowed whole.

Vultures

Vultures, known affectionately among the soldiers as shitehawks, because of their habit of feeding on dead animals, were to be seen in flimsy nests of sticks built in tall trees. They were large birds, often thought of as ugly, but with a kind of magnificent beauty all their own.

The Africans had a legend about this bird's behaviour. During the wet season, the vulture says to himself, 'When it stops raining I must build a house'. But when the rain stops, he says, 'When it rains again, I will build a house'. So the house never gets built.

Scorpions

Scorpions were to be found everywhere, especially in dark corners, and were very dangerous. They were around two to six inches long, with a hard, black shell-like body and comparatively enormous claws. They moved slowly, but were vicious when disturbed, quickly opening their claws and speedily snapping them together again with enough strength to penetrate a soldier's boot.

Attached to the victim in this way, the scorpion then brought up its tail and pressed its sting into its prey. The poison in the sting was enough to make a man faint immediately from shock and to remain ill for many days. When cornered, the creature killed itself with its own sting.

Hornets

British soldiers might have compared the African hornets with the wasps they knew from home. The hornet was as common in Africa as the wasp was in England, and the two creatures were similar, but the sting from the hornet was a lot more venomous than its British cousin.

Its nest, resembling that of a wasp, was built in mud and it flew on transparent wings in a clumsy but silent way, with its sting and legs hanging below its body.

Mosquitoes

Contrary to popular belief, mosquitoes fed on nectar, rather than human blood. However, the females of some species drank human blood for its nutrients and as an aid to developing their eggs. At the same time, these tiny insects would inject saliva that contained an anti-coagulant to prevent their proboscis from getting clogged with dried blood. They were responsible for spreading diseases such as malaria, prevented as much as possible by the soldiers having to sleep under mosquito nets every night.

Praying mantises

The praying mantis was an insect, so called because its front legs were held at an angle that appeared to be one of prayer. Although not dangerous to humans, they were formidable predators among the moths, crickets, grasshoppers, flies and other insects on which they fed. A triangular head, capable of revolving through 180 degrees, held two large compound eyes, capable of detecting fast movement, with three other simple eyes between them, capable of detecting only light and dark. Their legs were equipped with spikes that snared their prey, faster than the human eye could detect it, and held it in place, their reflexes so fast that passing insects stood little chance of escape. They also ate others of their own kind, and the female of the species was known for eating her mate during, or immediately after, mating.

Migratory birds

Strangely, some of the birds would have been familiar to the British, since they had migrated from Europe. Swallows and wagtails in particular arrived during October and stayed through to the following March or April, before flying north again on their return to Europe.

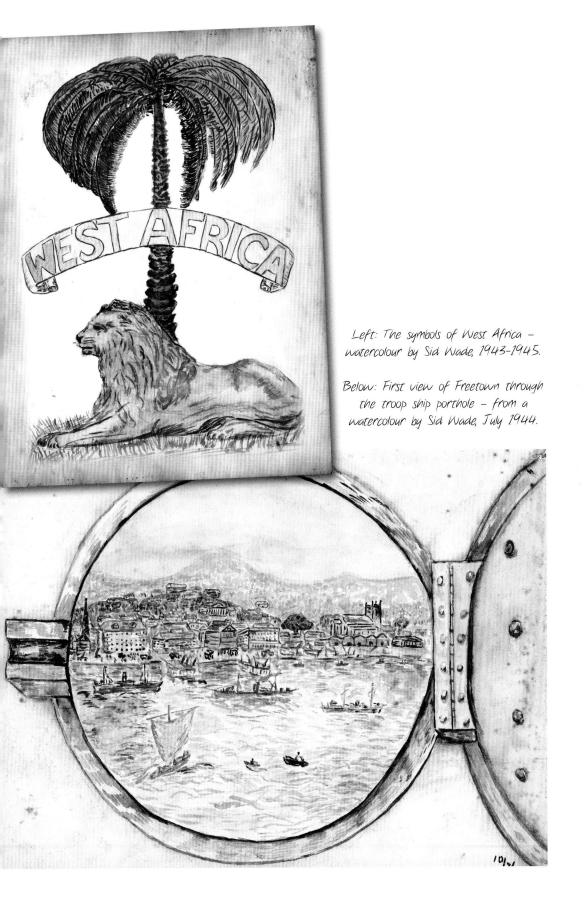

Left: The symbols of West Africa –
watercolour by Sid Wade, 1943-1945.

Below: First view of Freetown through
the troop ship porthole – from a
watercolour by Sid Wade, July 1944.

Left: View from a barrack room, overlooking Freetown Harbour – from a watercolour by Sid Wade, June 1944.

Below: Barrack room pastimes – cigarettes, darts and books – from a watercolour by Sid Wade, October 1944.

Above: Mosquito nets, soldiers for the sleeping under – from a watercolour by Sid Wade, May 1944.

Right: African boats and palms – watercolour by Sid Wade, May 1944.

Left: A memory of home – watercolour by Sid Wade, March 1944.

Right: Old sailing ships – watercolour by Sid Wade, April 1944. (Ships of this type, some-times known as argosies, seem to have been of special interest to Sid. A decade after the war ended, he opened his own printing business, which he called Argosy Reproductions.)

Left: Goats on the beach watercolour by Sid Wade, June 1944.

Right: The back of the barracks – watercolour by Sid Wade, June 1944.

Kissy Street, Freetown – a hand-tinted photograph.

Lumley Beach Road – a hand-tinted photograph.

Top; Bird's-eye view of Freetown and the harbour – a hand-tinted photograph.

Middle: Goderich Bay, Sierra Leone – a hand-tinted photograph.

Bottom: Water Street Avenue, Freetown – a hand-tinted photograph.

This page:

Above: Rokeh Bay, Sierra Leone — a hand-tinted photograph.

Left: Child farm worker — a hand-tinted photograph.

Opposite page:

Top: Central view of Freetown — a hand-tinted photograph.

Bottom: On the water at Waterloo — a hand-tinted photograph.

Fisher Street, Freetown – a hand-tinted photograph.

Lumley Beach – a hand-tinted photograph.

Ceremonies, Beliefs And Superstitions

The Africans who mingled with the British soldiers were in the midst of a culture shock in which the modern world continually clashed with their traditional ways and beliefs. Soldiers would hear tales about tribes where cannibalism and human sacrifice were still practised but, by the time of World War II, these stories were mostly apocryphal.

Charms and ju-ju

The Africans used charms as a protection against every kind of misfortune. The charm might be nothing more than a stone, but it would be one that was reputed to have been endowed with supernatural powers ascribed to ju-ju, a word that originated in West Africa and was derived from the French word 'joujou', meaning toy.

A conjurer and dancer perform for the crowd.

Other charms might take the form of a bird's beak, the skin of a chameleon, the horn of an antelope, the tail of a porcupine, the claw of a lion or nothing more than a bundle of feathers.

In the Nigerian Government Colliery miners kept their charms with them at all times and put as much faith in their ju-ju as they did in official safety devices.

Religious beliefs

In varying degrees many of the Africans still believed in witchcraft and magic. Despite this, and stories of religion being used as a cover for activities such as cannibalism and other unsavoury practices, the Africans, for the most part, were deeply religious.

They held a belief in a Supreme Being which existed in the trees, air, stones and rivers. They also believed in lesser gods who served the Supreme Being. They believed too in the spirits of ancestors, that the spirit of a dead person lived for a short time in a spiritual world before returning to earth in human form.

These beliefs often made funeral ceremonies and customs extremely elaborate, with the intention of ensuring that the spirit of the dead person would be happy in the spiritual world, as well as successful in its reincarnation.

When buried, a man would be placed on his left side facing the rising sun. This was because a man was said to rest more peacefully when he could see the rising sun calling him to his farm. A woman would be buried on her right side, facing the setting sun. It was thought that she would be more content when her eyes looked towards the sunset, beckoning her to prepare the evening meal. Both would be buried with a hand placed under a cheek.

In many ways the beliefs and some of the ceremonies practised by the Africans were not so far removed from Christian beliefs. When the Portuguese landed on the Gold Coast in the late 19th century, they celebrated a mass dedicated to St Christopher, the patron saint of travellers. When the watching Africans saw this, they were so impressed that they incorporated much of the observed mass into their own pagan rites. By the time of World War II, certain African events in this region were still celebrated with an almost exact replica of a Catholic mass. The main difference was that the African version included the sacrifice of a dog.

The British soldiers would also have seen their own God in the Africans' Supreme Being, along with a joint belief in an afterlife. The Africans even had something akin to the Christian Ten Commandments, albeit only five of them, which were taught to initiates of a religious society:

Respect and obey your father and mother.

When you are married, do not ill-treat your wife, and never meddle in her or other people's quarrels.

*To kill in war is to defend oneself and show valour,
but to kill at other times is to imitate the beasts.*

*Stealing is undignified. If you covet a thing,
ask for it. If it is refused, go without it.*

*Gambling is exciting, but it is precarious. What
you lose might give comfort to your family.*

The power of the drum

Part of African folklore decreed that the drummer was one of the first beings to be created by the Creator, and drums played a major role in the African's life.

Down through the ages, drums had been used to summon people to palavers, warn them of the approach of danger, direct them on the battlefield and bring them news from the outside world. Drums had beaten a heady rhythm for their joyful dances and aided their mourning at funerals. Drums had added dignity and solemnity to tribal gatherings and religious ceremonies.

Drums had their own language, interpreted by high or low notes, rapid or slow beats. Those that understood them had to have a particularly good ear for the nuances of the sound and the beat, but also to be a master of the vernacular of drum 'language'.

Drums played an important role in the Africans' lives.

Left: Beating the tom-tom.

Below: Tribal flogging – as illustrated in a government pamphlet.

The design of each drum varied according to the purpose it was intended to serve, but the basic principles of its construction were much the same, comprising a hollowed-out log with an animal skin or elephant ear stretched across it and held tautly in place with twine or pegs.

Drums were frequently worshipped in the belief that they contained the spirit of the trees from which they were carved. To appease the spirits, offerings of palm wine, fowl or eggs were made at the time that trees would be felled to be made into drums. Additionally, a prayer was offered that no misfortune should befall the people who cut down the tree, carved the drum, beat the drum or danced to its music.

In some parts of West Africa there was a belief that the man in the moon was the god of all drummers. When the moon was full, it was said, it was possible to see him holding his drumsticks over a drum. When he dropped the sticks on the drum, somewhere a drummer died.

Drums were decorated with many different charms and talismans. Often they took the form of human bones or those of a lion or gorilla. If human, then the bones must have belonged to someone of importance and won in battle.

Human sacrifices were once offered to drums, a tradition that lived on a little less gruesomely with the substitution of dog flesh, fowls, eggs, wine or newly acquired European drinks.

Drummers were always carefully selected for their roles and served an apprenticeship. When they died, their souls were believed to inhabit all drums.

Endurance tests

In some tribes, even by this time, the spirit and endurance of young men was tested by flogging. Stripped to the waist and with his arms held above his head, the young man was required to accept blows from a cane wielded by the tribe's official flogger. The ceremony was watched by eager spectators as the flogger and flogged circled one another, the flogger making feints with his cane so the person taking the blows never knew when the next one would strike. Blood frequently flowed and canes often broke as the youth received a total of twenty-one blows. In another variation of the ceremony, two youths would flog each other.

The site of Creation?

A year before the outbreak of World War II, archaeologists discovered a number of bronze heads at the Nigerian city of Ife, now home to the Natural History Museum of Nigeria. It was this city that the Yoruba people believed to be the scene of the Creation. The story, handed down by word of mouth from generation to generation, was that originally the world was covered with water, but the Lord of Heaven sent down a priest called Ojumu with a supply of magic sand. Ojumu threw the sand, which was spread by a five-fingered fowl, also sent by the Lord of Heaven. Dry land appeared and the Lord of Heaven instructed Odua to descend and establish a kingdom.

Odua descended to the earth by a chain to a place where Ife now stands. He was accompanied by sixteen elders and their followers, one of whom, Orisha, then fashioned men and women.

Interestingly, much more modern thinking today has identified Africa as the place where mankind first developed.

Rest And Recreation

L ife in the White Man's Grave wasn't all bad. Off duty, Sid and his fellow soldiers could swim at a place called Lumley Beach, or have a drink at nearby Paddy's Bar. Founded by Irishman Paddy Warren, the bar was rare in the fact that it stayed open right through World War II. (Paddy died in 2005, and his famous bar, very different now to what it was then to the British soldiers of World War II, has become one of the top nightspots for tourists to Freetown. Likewise, Lumley Beach today is a luxury holiday resort.)

The Creek at Lumley Beach, where the soldiers spent much of their leisure time.

When posted to a unit in the bush, there was the opportunity for big game hunting, with hippopotamus, leopards and deer on offer. Sid's pacifist attitudes prevented him from shooting wild animals, although he did possess a crocodile skin briefcase with a strange gouge in the front of it. He liked to tell everyone that it was where he shot the crocodile that the case had been made from, but it was far more likely that he had bought it in Freetown's open market.

When the soldiers weren't swimming or visiting hole in the wall bars run by Syrians to drink gin or red wine out of jam jars, they would go to the NAAFI to listen to Sid playing the *Warsaw Concerto* or accompanying them in songs they had written themselves. The words dealt in no uncertain terms with the cheerful misery of their daily lives, or how the best view of the coast would be from the stern-end of a troop ship, taking them home and back to England.

Church services and other entertainments

Freetown's St George's Cathedral wasn't the only place of worship for the soldiers. On Whit Sunday, 28th May 1944, the Tower Hill Garrison Church was opened and dedicated by the Right Reverend JLC Horstead, Lord Bishop of Sierra Leone. Its purpose was to be used, not just for worship, but for other cultural activities too. Here's what a programme, issued at the time of the dedication, said on the matter:

> It is intended to put this Church, for the benefit of people in the Tower Hill area, to many uses.
>
> Primarily, it will be for Divine Worship and Private Prayer – a place to which men may go and receive grace and gain strength. It will also be used for those things pertaining to the Glory of God which are of a Democratic, Social, or Cultural interest to many. As an expression of our belief that religion, politics and life are inseparable, we see no reason why, with due regard to the sacredness of the building, lectures, concerts, plays and discussions of a high level should not take place within the House of God. Possibly in future our churches will be used more for these things; at least this is a fair and carefully planned experiment.
>
> Whosoever thou art that enterest this Church, may God be with you, guide you, bless you, and keep you always.

Within three days of that dedication service, the church was being put to good use as the venue for a music concert, with members of the forces singing solos and performing piano, flute and violin works by composers that included Bach, Brahms, Chopin, Handel, Schubert, Glazunov, Delius, Vaughan Williams, Debussy and Grieg.

DEDICATION OF TOWER HILL GARRISON CHURCH

by

Rt. Rev. J. L. C. Horstead, M.A., Lord Bishop of Sierra Leone

on

Whit Sunday, 28th May, at 9-30 a.m.

———— ✦ ·· ● ·· ✦ ————

Order of Service

Voluntary
Concerto in D Minor (slow movement). *Bach*

The Petition
" Reverend Father in God we pray you dedicate this Church."
Bishop.—" I am ready to proceed to the Dedication."

The Entrance
The Bishop, taking his Pastoral Staff, shall knock three times on the closed door.
" Peace be to this house from God."
   Hymn, A. & M. 747.
The Hymn ended, the Bishop shall say (the people standing)
" Let us Pray."
After a prayer he will proceed with :—

The Benedictions
   Hymn 242, verses 1 and 2, shall be sung.
Then shall the Bishop, laying his hand on the Font, Bless the same.
   Hymn 242, verse 3, shall be sung.
Then shall the Bishop, laying his hand on the Altar, Bless the same.
   Hymn 242, verse 4, shall be sung.
Then shall the Bishop, laying his hand on the Lectern and Pulpit, Bless the same.
   Hymn 242, verse 5, shall be sung.
Then shall the Bishop, laying his hand on the Reading Desk, Bless the same.
   Hymn 242, verse 6, shall be sung.
Then shall the Bishop, laying his hand on the Ornaments and Vessels, Bless the same.
   Hymn 242, verse 7, shall be sung.

The First Lesson
1. Chronicles, 29, 1 - 13.   Read by Major-General C. G. Philips, D.S.O., M.C.
The Psalm 150.

The Second Lesson
Hebrews, 10, 19 - 25.   Read by Rev. W. Farrer, Deputy Assistant Chaplain-General, W.A.

The Dedication
Hymn 157.
The congregation will kneel and the Bishop will proceed to Dedicate the Building.
Then shall follow The Lord's Prayer.
Hymn 154.

The Sermon
Hymn 604.
The Blessing.

THE NATIONAL ANTHEM

Voluntary
Sonata in G Major (second movement). *Bach*.

There will follow a Celebration of Holy Communion for all who like to stay.

———— ✦ ·· ● ·· ✦ ————

Thanks are due to all those who, in one way or another,
have helped or contributed to making this a House of God.
Further assistance in beautifying it will be appreciated.

Order of service for the dedication of Tower Hill Garrison Church, 28th May 1944.

It is interesting to speculate on whether the preference of classical music over popular songs of the day was a result of the concert being held in a church, or whether the men really preferred classical works. Whatever the reason, the fact is that classical music predominated in concerts at the venue. Likewise, lectures, discussions and the like were always of a serious, rather than a frivolous nature.

A glance through the church's programme of events for the period between 28th May and 31st October 1944 shows a predominance of religious services, but also lectures on subjects such as The Siege of Tobruk, Russia, Primitive Art and Twenty-five Years Experiences of a Soldier in West Africa; discussions on topics that included housing after the war, employment after the war, education after the war, politics after the war and Germany after the war; plus plenty of community singing, musical evenings and radiogram concerts.

Somewhat smaller than St George's Cathedral, the village church on the road to Lumley Beach.

Seeing the funny side

This was not to say that the soldiers were short of a sense of humour, willing to poke fun at themselves, the army in general and even religion. Spurred on no doubt by the convoluted way in which the army listed stores – not *soldiers' army boots*, but *boots, army, soldiers for the use of* – a group of the men got together to produce a satirical document, listing personnel, transport and equipment purporting to be from the Spiritual Aid Detachment, designed to deal with 200 sinners per day. Among the required personnel were:

Samaritan, Grade 1
Interpreters, Writing Wall
Fitters, wing
Fitters, halo
Whiteners, sepulchre
Virgins, foolish
Virgins, wise

Transport listed included:

Chariots, fiery
Clouds, ascending
Arks, collapsible, rainproof

Other needed equipment comprised:

Pearls, castable
Paths, straight
Paths, narrow
Boxes, manna
Doves, turtle
Crooks, shepherds
Lamps, virgin, wise, filled
Lamps, virgin, foolish, empty
Chains, retaining, body and soul

Bottles, wine, old (for new wine)
Bows, rain
Calves, fatted
Gates, pearly, left
Gates, pearly, right
Walls, collapsible, Jericho pattern
Cymbals, loud
Cymbals, well-tuned
Baskets, rush, infants
Rushes, bull
Trumpets, archangel, brazen
Slings, David pattern
Lightning, with fork
Lightning, with sheet
Leaves, fig concealing
Loaves, five
Fishes, small
Wine, new (for bottles, old)
Branches, olive
Locusts, dried
Honey, wild
Commandments, sorted, packets of ten

Amateur dramatics

During May and June 1944, some of the men, calling themselves The New England Repertory Company staged a play called *Youth at the Helm* at the Tower Hill Theatre. In some ways, it was a strange choice for British forces to be performing, since it was originally written in German by a playwright named Paul Vulpius. It was, however, translated and adapted by English playwright Hubert Griffith, one of several plays that he similarly adapted from the work of Vulpius, and it seems to have been taken to the hearts of the British. It was performed at the Westminster Repertory Theatre in London's Westminster in 1934 and again at The Globe Theatre in 1935, each time starring Alastair Sim; broadcast on television in 1938, at a time when British TV was in its infancy; and was even staged during the war, in November and December 1943, at Birmingham Repertory Theatre.

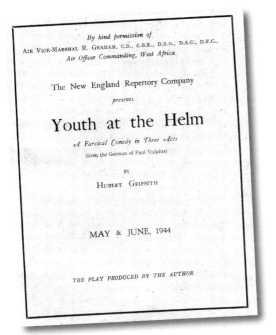

By kind permission of
Air Vice-Marshal R. Graham, C.B., C.B.E., D.S.O., D.S.C., D.F.C.,
Air Officer Commanding, West Africa

The New England Repertory Company

presents

Youth at the Helm

A Farcical Comedy in Three Acts
(from the German of Paul Vulpius)

BY

Hubert Griffith

MAY & JUNE, 1944

THE PLAY PRODUCED BY THE AUTHOR

The programme for Youth at the Helm, performed during May and June 1944.

Youth at the Helm, despite its German origins, was in fact a very typical English kind of farce, concerning a young unemployed man who walks into the London and Metropolitan bank one day and installs himself at a vacant desk. He acts as though he is an employee and begins writing business letters to various concerns. No one else there likes to admit they don't know who he is and so he is left unchallenged.

The African version had a cast of thirteen, backed up by three stage staff and an electrician. Incidental music, supplied by gramophone records once again showed a predilection for classical music, with works by the likes of Tchaikovsky, Delibes, Strauss, Mozart and Ponchielli. What made the servicemen in Africa choose this particular play was perhaps due to the fact that it was produced by the author, Hubert Griffith, whom it must be assumed was stationed in Sierra Leone at the time. Elsewhere, a group calling themselves The Garrison Players staged a production of *The Man Who Changed His Name* by Edgar Wallace. Despite being performed in a disease-ridden, tropical land, the very English action of the play took place in Ascot during the summer of 1939.

Artists and photographers

Sid Wade, as has been noted before, was not a particularly enthusiastic soldier, but he was an enthusiastic artist – not a great artist, but a competent one in watercolour paintings and pencil drawings. He wasn't alone. Several of his barrack room buddies were equally proficient with pencil, pen, paint and paper.

He and many of his fellow soldiers were also enthusiastic photographers, keen to make a record of the people and their surroundings, even though the cameras available to them were capable of little more than snapshots.

Some of the soldiers' paintings, drawings and photographs are shown in the following two chapters.

Newsletters

Soldiers from Tower Hill Barracks researched, wrote and published their own newsletter. Initially called *The Bugle*, its purpose, according to the editor, was to 'provide amusement and news of an exclusive nature whenever possible'. *The Bugle* consisted of around eight pages of typed foolscap (the standard paper size that predated today's A4), containing an eclectic mix of hard news about the war, together with football fixtures, sports reports and birthday wishes to readers. Also included were film reviews, short jokes, longer humorous pieces, church news, articles written about aspects of England that soldiers held dear and personal stories of African experiences.

The newsletter said a lot about the soldiers' way of life and way of thinking, as well as the depth of their knowledge on topics unrelated to their surroundings. In one article, a soldier gives an account of his home county of Essex, in which he explores the history of the county in a way worthy of any professional historian. (It is suspected, from the style of writing, the interest in history and the county in question that this was written by Sid Wade, who was listed among the editorial staff.) In another, a list of jokes are compiled that would have been worthy of Max Miller in those days. Intermingled with such light-hearted topics, the reader is plunged into a personal account of a battle with harrowing details of deaths. Then, just as suddenly, the newsletter switches to a humorous story by a soldier dreaming about going home and seeing his wife again, before moving into a religious sermon that compares Christianity with Communism.

With the June 1944 issue of the newsletter, its name was changed from *The Bugle* to *The Bullom*. The new name was chosen because of its association with Africa's West Coast – Bullom being the name of the Northern Province of Sierra Leone. With the new name came a more serious approach, with the occasional supplement dedicated exclusively to war cables from London to keep the soldiers informed about how the war was progressing in other parts of the world. Articles in the new newsletter were of a more factual nature with less emphasis on the frivolous.

Considering that the soldiers put the newsletters together completely in their own time, and with a lack of journalistic experience, the wealth of information and entertainment they provided was remarkable. Equally impressive was the quality of the writing and editing, and while there were instances of foreign place names being incorrectly spelt, the newsletters were near enough grammatically perfect.

For the price of threepence (a little over 1p in today's decimal coinage), they offered much welcome information and entertainment to the soldiers.

Two later chapters reprint in full an issue each of *The Bugle* and *The Bullom* as they appeared in 1944.

The Bugle and The Bullom — newsletters produced by the soldiers in 1944.

Army Artists

Painting and drawing were popular pastimes for many of the soldiers. Whether they used watercolours, pencils or pen and ink, their artwork mainly captured their surroundings, with occasional diversions into pictures of home or other imaginary subjects, painted or drawn from memory. Some were very professional, others rather amateurish, but regardless of the level of proficiency – or lack of it – the pictures the soldiers produced give a greater insight into their thoughts and the place they had found themselves in than words ever could. Here are some examples of their artwork.

Left: The bush, anywhere in Africa – pencil drawing by Sid Wade, November 1944.

Right: Four Mile Point – pencil drawing by Sid Wade, January 1944.

Banana Gate entrance to Tower Hill
Barracks – pencil drawing by Sid
Wade, December 1944.

Road through the bush – pen and
ink drawing by unknown soldier.

Right: Portrait
of an African –
crayon drawing
by unknown
soldier.

Left: Portrait
of Sid –
pencil drawing
by unknown
soldier.

English fashion at home – pen and ink
drawing by unknown soldier.

An African Photo Album

The photo album that follows is made up of two different types of photograph: professional and amateur. The professional pictures are from original photographic postcards produced and published by two photographers known as the Lisk-Carew brothers. Alphonso and Arthur Lisk-Carew ran studios out of their house and at their business premises, both in Freetown, advertising themselves as photographers, importers of photographic materials, stationery, toys and fancy goods. The brothers shot hundreds of pictures in and around Sierra Leone many of which were turned into postcards that were bought by the soldiers. They were available along with smaller, hand-tinted pictures, which were sold as souvenirs. The Lisk-Carew studios were also visited by the soldiers to have formal pictures taken of themselves in their tropical kit, as mementos of their time abroad.

Left: A Sanderson plate camera, the type of model that would have been used in the Lisk-Carew studios at this time.

Right: Soldiers were likely to be using simple box cameras or folding models like these for their amateur snapshots.

The amateur pictures were taken by the soldiers, using film bought and developed at the Lisk-Carew studio. While the quality of their pictures does not match that of the professional photographers, their approach to the subjects, as is so often the case with simple snapshots, is more emotive, especially when viewed this far removed from the days when they were taken. The soldiers would have been using amateur box cameras or, at the best, simple folding models, and their photography was hampered by several conditions. As any professional photographer knows, the best time to take pictures is when the sun is low in the sky early or late in the day. When the sun is overhead during the middle of the day, it casts harsh, unattractive shadows and destroys details in a subject's texture.

Freetown's geographic position, less than 600 miles from the equator, meant that the sun was overhead for most of the day, and therefore rarely conducive to shooting good quality pictures. The contrast of the dark skin of the African people against such brilliantly lit backgrounds also led to lack of detail in many subjects.

And yet, if the viewer is prepared to look beyond the often low quality of the pictures and the problems faced by the amateur photographers, the pictures they produced say as much about day to day life for the troops as the most professional of pictures ever could.

The professional pictures which follow are captioned from information on the original postcards and other images. The amateur, uncaptioned pictures represent a mix of subjects that simply appealed to the now unknown soldiers who shot them.

Professional pictures by the Lisk-Carew brothers

Looking out over Freetown to the harbour.

Freetown Harbour, home to many different types of boat.

Dug out canoes, a popular form of water transport.

Mafulomoo, Sierra Leone.

Native houses line the shores of a lagoon.

Climbing an oil palm.

Sail boats in the early evening.

Palm wine distiller, Sierra Leone.

The incongruity of a white suited man
with straw boater in a jungle clearing.

Charlotte Falls, Sierra Leone.

A busy waterway outside Freetown.

The railway line to Waterloo.

One of the better bridges through the Bush.

Cooking at an open air fireside.

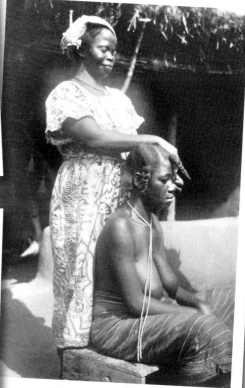

Lining up to cross the river
by a precarious bridge.

The art of hair plaiting.

An outdoor kitchen in Freetown.

A mother pounds grain, as she
smokes a pipe and nurses her baby.

A tribal ceremony about to begin.

Taking part in a masquerade.

An acrobat performs for the crowd.

A small community of native houses.

Masked children take part in their own ceremony.

A large ant hill.

Amateur pictures by soldiers

The Sierra Leone Bugle

THE
SIERRA LEONE
BUGLE

SIERRA LEONE'S
BRIGHTEST,
BREEZIEST PAPER

EDITORIAL
OFFICES:

TOWER HILL
BARRACKS,
SIERRA LEONE

Vol 3 No.9   Monday 29 May 1944   Price threepence

GOOD PROGRESS IN ITALY

Our troops have now broken out of the Anzio bridgehead. Fifth Army troops have taken the town of Cori, seven miles north-east of Cisterna and eight miles from the main road between Naples and Rome, via Cassino and the Liri valley. Advanced elements are reported to be approaching Valmontini, which lies on this highway itself.

Allied troops are also reported within a short distance of Velletri which is only twenty miles due south of Rome.

On the northern flank of the bridgehead the enemy is reported to be strengthening his position around Carrocoto, presumably, to prevent a further Allied thrust towards Rome.

On the main front, steady progress is being made in the hills to the south of the Pontine Marshes and along the River Liri. A height eight miles north of Cassino, which dominates the Liri valley, has been captured.

Canadian troops distinguished themselves in overcoming stubborn enemy resistance when the Eighth Army broke through the Adolf Hitler line.

The Royal Navy has given splendid support during the week by bombarding enemy shore positions along the Italian coast.

The ME Air Force has kept up a sustained attack on the

enemy positions, airfields
railway communications and
other objectives.

BURMA AND THE FAR EAST

Our troops have sealed off
all approaches to Myitkyina
and all attempts by the Japs
to counter attack have been
defeated.

In Assam, the enemy
attempts to capture Imphal
have all been frustrated.

Chinese troops are advancing
southward into Burma.

The enemy is withdrawing
from the Maffin Bay Airfield
in New Guinea.

WESTERN EUROPE

On Wednesday night, the RAF
carried out a heavy raid on
Aachen, a railway centre of
great importance on the line
leading from Germany to the
Channel Ports, and Mosquitoes
also bombed Berlin which had
a heavy daylight raid on
Wednesday.

There has been relatively
little enemy activity over
Britain of late.

FOOTBALL FIXTURES

29 May, REME v Bandages at
Brookfields.1 June, Bandages v
REME at Transit Camp.

5 June, Bandages v ESP at
Transit Camp.

TOWER HILL GARRISON CHURCH

The new Tower Hill Garrison
Church was opened and Dedicated on Whit Sunday, 28th May
1944.

In the words of Padre
Worsley, the Church will be

for Divine Worship and Private
Prayer. It will also be used
for those things which are
of a Democratic, Social, or
Cultural interest to many.

A splendid programme along
those lines has been arranged
and it is generally felt that
Padre Worsley's efforts will
fill a gap, the need of which,
has long been felt.

Below we reproduce the
programme for the next
fortnight:-

Sun 28 May

0930 Dedication of the new
     Church by the Right
     Reverend The Bishop of
     Sierra Leone.
1015 Communion Service.
2000 Community Singing.
2030 Evening Service.

Wed 31 May

2000 A Concert arranged by
Captain H Denton.

Thurs 1 Jun

2000 Lecture by Mr AB
Matthews, Public Relations
Officer.

Sun 4 Jun

0800 Communion.
0915 Morning Service.
2000 Community singing.
2030 Evening Service.

Wed 7 June

2000 Lecture by Major GW
Wellington.

PERSONALITIES BY THE "STROLLER"

Birthdays
Happy Birthday to Chief
Mechanician CE Hall (Escort
Force) for 6th June. He will
be 42. Also to Lieutenant

Corporal Alan Cooke, (Movement Control) for 14th June. Alan will be 22.

Sincere greetings to Sergeant HA Dean (R.E.) for 24th June. He will be 30.

FatherAB WH Inglis (Escort Force) has received the news that he has become a father. The new arrival is a boy. Our congratulations.

HOSPITAL

Stoker H Morgan (RN) is in hospital and is showing signs of progress. Sergeant KJ Davies (Line Sect) and Corporal Woods (Signals) are both in hospital.

STORY OF A HERO

'B' Company was the first to land at Salerno and had a definite objective to get. This objective was vital and, come what may, they had to get there. Heavy opposition was met with and the first encounter with the enemy resulted in one platoon suffering heavy casualties. However, they pressed on and finally gained their objective but were counter-attacked.

A hand-to-hand battle followed in which they were outnumbered. The commander rallied his men and, using his own words, 'fairly sorted 'em out'. The enemy had the advantage in number and drove the tired infantrymen back. The situation seemed, indeed, hopeless as a fresh platoon came up to reinforce them and, with some remnants from other regiments, the commander reorganised his forces, just in time to repel another enemy attack.

For the next five hours, pitched battle was fought. The enemy attacked with their infantry and their tanks. But the British tommy is not easily beaten and, springing forward like panthers, they counter attacked and drove the enemy off and knocked out two of their tanks. To do this many officers and men lost their lives. Orders are orders in warfare, the company had to hold on.

Eventually 'B' Company was relieved and the objective consolidated by the Guards, who had landed later in the day. It had been a close call.

The company of infantrymen had done a great and gallant job.

Next day, the commander, who was the only officer left of the company, visited the scene of action and there found all his men who had died so gallantly.

Among these heroes was one, Private Jim Inglis. He had been killed by an automatic weapon. Near him were three Panzer Grenadiers - one shot and two bayoneted. He had not died alone, the evidence was around him. He scorned the word 'impossible'. He did not know the meaning of the word 'fear'.

'He died like a very gallant gentleman,' wrote his captain to his brother Seaman WH Inglis, serving on one of HM ships now in port in West Africa.

WERE YOU BORN IN MAY?

The Emerald - the birthstone
of the May-born is one of
the oldest and most precious
stones. It is prized today as
much as it was three thousand
years ago when, because of
its rare beauty and colour,
the Egyptians considered it a
stone of the Gods.

In those days, sacred
images had flashing emerald
eyes. Later, the Mohammedans,
believed that a rough emerald
inscribed with a verse of
the Koran was a talisman
of immortality. They also
regarded this gem as a
symbol of constancy and true
affection - a superstition
which still exists today.

The highly polished emerald
was said to have the power
of restoring failing sight.
Shakespeare, describing the
emerald, says:

*The deep green emerald in
whose fresh regard*

*Weak sights their sickly
radiance do renew.*

And Nero, watching the
contest of gladiators in his
palace, used an emerald eye-
glass to lengthen his vision.

The emerald is also
a talisman of sailors.
Suspended round their neck
so that the gem lies against
the breast, an uncut emerald
is supposed to preserve
fishermen and those that
work on the sea from perils
and misfortunes. It is also
the stone of adventure and
travel, many famous explorers
being born in May.

●

EDGAR WALLACE PLAY PRESENTED BY GARRISON PLAYERS

The Man Who Changed His Name
by Edgar Wallace is being
presented by the Tower Hill
Garrison Players to units in
Sierra Leone.

The play is directed by
Major Patrick Campbell who
also plays the role of Frank
O'Ryan. Sheila Peate, plays
the part of Nita Clive, the
wife of Selby Clive played by
Kenneth Sharpe, the 'man who
changed his name'. The diction
is clear and the players
give life and reality to the
characters with which they are
entrusted.

In a different sphere are
Ray Cox as Lane and Captain
Harold Denton as Sir Ralph
Whitcombe, KC Al Gentry gives
a good impression of the
American, Jerry Muller.

The action of the play is
in the drawing room of a lodge
near Ascot, in the summer of
1939.

SAYINGS

*Life is just one thing after
another - and love is just
two things after each other.*

AT YOUR LOCAL

The Moon is Down

20th Century Fox paid $60,000
for the film rights of John
Steinbeck's *The Moon is Down*.
The film is disappointing
and Sir Cedric Hardwicke
as the Nazi Colonel is
unrealistic and is the most
English character which

Hollywood has ever produced. The scene of the film is Norway and it could be of any conquered country. Its theme, that a brave people are unconquerable.

Stage Door Canteen

Here is a picture guaranteed to chase away the blues. It is served up lavishly in one gigantic dish. Charlie McCarthy, Gracie Fields and Zehudi Menuhin are in the cast. The film is based on the canteen founded by the American Theatre Wing in New York for service men. There's music, singing and dancing.

Dear Octopus

Dodie Smith's London stage success has been translated into a likeable, refreshing film. The story pictures life in an English country house when members of a large family re-unite to celebrate a golden wedding. Margaret Lockwood and Michael Wilding are the stars.

Hangmen Also Die

A film dealing with the old story of Gestapo brutality and the sufferings and sacrifices of the unhappy people of countries occupied by the Nazis. The assassination of Heydrich, known as the Butcher, starts the story. Unable to find the patriot who killed him, the Gestapo introduce their acts of terrorism. The Quisling traitor is magnificently portrayed by Gene Lockhart and Brian Donlevy gives an

excellent performance as the killer of Heydrich. Walter Brennan, as a professor and patriot, and Anna Lee, as his daughter, give sterling support.

Dixie

Bing Crosby comes to the screen again to entertain you with a fresh batch of songs.

JACK JESTER'S CHEERY CHATTER

To help you smile, and while you smile another smiles.

Thought for the Week: The surest way to wash out friendship is to sponge on it.

Did you hear about the two boys who were very much alike? 'Twins?' asked the billeting officer. 'No, Sir,' said the lads in unison. When he filled in their forms he noted they gave the same birthday. 'But you said you weren't twins' he exclaimed. 'We ain't, sir. We were triplets.'

'Now don't worry about your wife,' said the doctor, 'You'll have a different woman when she gets back from hospital.' 'Yes, I know, but what if she finds out, doc?' said the husband.

Before the war, women went without pastry to get thin. Now they go without it because they can't get fat.

A sister with a touch of influenza, took with her to a party two handkerchiefs, one of which she stuck in her bosom. At supper she began rummaging to right and left in her bosom for the fresh handkerchief. Engrossed in her search, she suddenly realized that conversation had ceased and people were watching her, fascinated. In confusion she murmured, 'I know I had two when I came.'

The volunteer driver of a train on the local railway had performed the remarkable feat of bringing the train in thirty-five minutes ahead of schedule. The European and native passengers went forward in a body to compliment him. A face emerged from the cab. 'Don't thank me', he gasped, 'Thank God. I only found out how to stop the b····y thing ten minutes ago.'

Wasted energy is telling a hair-raising story to a bald-headed man.

I know an architect who went on the halls but still kept drawing poor houses.

Two shipwrecked Scotsmen, after managing to swim to an isolated rock, there found their position becoming perilous. By agreement, one of them was about to offer a prayer to the Almighty, promising to contribute £5 to charity if they were rescued. Just as he was about to make the petition, the other, scanning the distant horizon, shouted, 'Stop, Jock, don't commit yourself. I think I can see a sail.'

A Scotsman entered a train going towards Daru and was told by the guard that he was in the wrong compartment. He went to another portion, to be told that he was wrong again. Swearing at everybody, he entered another carriage and a padre said, 'Young man, do you know you are going straight to hell.' 'Oh heck,' said Jock, 'I'm on the wrong b····y train.'

Cheerfully Yours,
Jack Jester

BEAUTY SPOTS OF ENGLAND - ESSEX

The charm of Essex scenery is a never failing series of surprises to those who explore it for the first time.

The wealth of historical association is not surprising when we remember how often and prominently, for over 2,000 years, this corner of East Anglia has figured in successive chapters of our island story. The Romans established one of their first and most important colonies here, the Saxons, the Norsemen, the Danes and the Normans all, in succession, found it much to their liking.

For many years after the Conquest, Essex was one of the wealthiest, most favoured and most pleasant parts of the Kingdom, seeing much of the comings and goings of kings, princes and nobles, for many of whom it was a favourite place of residence.

As a result almost every parish could boast of some connection with the outstanding events and commanding figures of history. The countryside became studded with royal lodges, massive castles, rich abbeys and priories, and some of the stateliest mansions in England, whose sites or ruins, abounding in past memories, make Essex an almost inexhaustible mine of legend and story.

Two of the oldest historic sites in the county are earthworks known as Ambresbury Banks and Loughton Camp, in the glorious sylvan setting of Epping Forest, which legend associates with Queen Boadicea. It has been established to the satisfaction of most historians that Essex was the scene of the exploits of the warrior queen who led the ancient Britons against the Roman invaders, and inflicted a number of severe defeats upon them. Her last and disastrous battle with the Roman general Suctonius, in which 80,000 of our brave but undisciplined ancestors were slain, was fought somewhere between Colchester and London.

Ambresbury Banks, with its roughly oval enclosure surrounded by a ditch and a rampart, lies just off the London-Epping road. About a mile or so to the south-east, near Loughton itself, in one of the highest and most beautiful parts of the Forest, is Loughton Camp.

In Colchester, the Roman Colonia Camulodunum, the county has one of the most important and interesting of all relics of the Roman occupation. Its chief pride is the massive Roman wall, still in great part intact, which, about ten feet high and eight foot thick, can be traced round much of the older part of the town.

The length of the wall - it measures over 3,000 yards - is evidence of the importance of this outpost of the Roman Empire. Camulodunum had the unusual privilege of its own mint, and many of the Roman coins found in immense quantities in Essex bear the mark C or Cl, indicating that they were minted locally. Among a large number of fascinating antiquities found, and now preserved in Colchester, are a tombstone bearing the effigy of a Roman centurion and a Roman alter, with inscriptions to the mother-goddesses of pagan belief.

Essex was the site also of the chief Roman fortress guarding the coast, Othona, remains of which are to be found near Bradwell Juxta Mare, the quaintly named township at the mouth of the Blackwater. This district, and the Essex coast and riverside as a whole, are perhaps more interesting, however, for their associations with the Saxons and later sea-rovers, who settled here in large numbers after the Romans withdrew.

One of the most interesting reminders of Saxons days is the church of St. Peter on the Wall, near Bradwell, on the site of the Roman station mentioned above. It is generally accepted as having been built by St. Cedd, the Christian missionary to the East Saxons, in 655, and if this is so it is the most ancient church in Essex and a link with the introduction of Christianity into our country.

Another especially interesting reminder of that period is St. Osyth's Priory, on the wide-stretching, breezy marshland close to Clacton. According to the most romantic legend, St. Osyth, locally pronounced 'Toosey', was the head of a Saxon nunnery who was beheaded by the Danes for refusing to worship their idols.

Thereafter, on one night of every year, the headless body of the murdered abbess walked the scene of her martyrdom, and when the house was refounded in 1118, the bones of the saint were enshrined in the new church.

The Thames-side marshes, intersected with numerous ditches or fleets as they are called locally, were well-suited to the long ships of the Danes and Norsemen, and many districts hereabouts have associations with their grim times. The ravaging Danes built one of their chief eyries on the hill above the church at South Benfleet (from which, incidentally, the modern visitor has magnificent views of the Thames estuary) and Alfred the Great fought a gory battle with them in the wastes around North Benfleet.

On occasion, of course, the Danes penetrated farther inland. They once sailed up the Thames, and then along the Lea, to pillage a religious house in Epping Forest, on the site of which Harold later founded Waltham Abbey. It was here that Alfred adroitly turned the tables on them by diverting the river and leaving them high and dry. Waltham Abbey is said to have been the burial place of Harold after the Battle of Hastings.

Altogether the Norman Barons built some eleven castles in Essex. That at Colchester built largely of material from the Roman ruins, is outstanding as the largest of all the Norman keeps now remaining in England, exceeding even that of the Tower of London, which it closely resembles. Castle Hedingham, on the northern boundary of the county, is also a fine and interesting Norman keep while Hadleigh has some grand and extensive ruins.

There were nearly fifty priories, abbeys and monasteries founded in Essex during the two centuries after the Conquest, and some of these remain today as picturesque and interesting reminders, including the abbey at Coggeshall, the recently carefully restored ruins of Beeleigh Abbey near Maldon and St Osyth's Priory already mentioned. It must not be thought, however, that Essex history is concerned only with kings, princes and nobles. It was at Fobbing, in one of the most desolate stretches of the Thames Marshes, that Jack Straw's rising began, following the introduction of the poll tax in the fourteenth century.

Essex men marched in their hundreds to Smithfield, there to be joined by the Kentish followers of Wat Tyler. Essex provided no small number of the Protestants who suffered at the stake for their beliefs during the reign of Queen Mary of Scots, and Brentwood (formerly Burntwood) on the main London-Colchester highway, can still show the stump of a tree at which many local martyrs were burned, as well as a monument erected to their memory when Protestantism was again the lawful doctrine.

Of such variety is Essex history made up, and although these notes have merely stretched a subject which could easily fill a volume, they will have justified themselves if they induce even a few readers to go exploring in the neglected county when 'unnecessary' journeying is again permissible.

THE PATENT'S DILEMMA

I was out! The transformation had taken just over three years. I was sent into hospital by Captain I Segal, Medical Officer at Tower Hill Barracks, who had been as busy as a one fingered clarinet player that day, 15th March 1944. I had epidermophytosis. Job had nothing on me. Spots, blemishes, pimples, irritation, soreness etc., etc. I was a dermatologist's dream come true.

My skin was saturated with over twenty types of ointments, with colours ranging from rich purple to chrome yellow. In hospital our multi-coloured faces were such that lights had to be dimmed in the auditorium before the ENSA show artists appeared on the stage. It was a tactful gesture and lessened the risk of shocking the cast. Most performances started with a full throated extempore chorus *My Bonny Has Got Dermatitis.*

My medical category soon dropped from A1 to A3 and then down to B7.

At mealtimes we sat agitatedly up on our beds and made desperate signals to the African orderlies who were as forgetful as absent-minded plumbers in love, to make sure we didn't get overlooked. Most patients were swathed in bandages and one in the next bed to mine looked like the invisible Man in the film.

The first signs of the promised land came when the Medical Officer, Captain S Jacobs, who was a born enthusiast on skin complaints and everything else he handled, with the Assistant Director of Medical Services, Colonel AJ Beveridge, MC, DSO, got together and, standing by my bed, said, 'He should be recommended for a board.' I opened my mouth to speak but the Medical Officer thrust a thermometer into it. The thermometer was withdrawn and he looked at it and said, 'Hmm'. Then he put on his stethoscope and listened through it to my chest. 'Say ninety-nine,' he requested. 'Ninety-nine,' I murmured. The Medical Officer repeated

'Hmm' and commenced to tap my chest with two fingers. Next morning I heard the awful outcome. I was to be given my ticket. Then the fun started. Ten forms had to be signed in duplicate, one form in triplicate. Medical History Affirmations, Dependants Allowances, Disclaimers, Cash Issues and several other forms were completed. I signed my name thirty-five times.

The questions were detailed and peculiar. When did you first contract this complaint? Did it ever occur in civilian life? Who treated you? How many times? Where? What in your opinion caused the complaint? What Army treatment have you had? How many hospitals have you attended? What is your medical category? Four hours later I met the Quartermaster, received £4.10s 0d in lieu of a ready-made suit and shook hands with Colonel HP Gabb MC, CO of the hospital.

I then went to say goodbye to my fellow patients from the ward.

All looked with wonder in their eyes, as I walked out of the hospital grounds. I left with 'E' tagged on the end of my name. I walked along contented and happy, with thoughts of freedom in my mind.

I arrived home tired after a long journey and after having a hurried meal, retired to bed. My wife followed soon after. She yawned and stretched her lithe youthful and pure white arms before the dressing table mirror. I looked at the boudoir clock beside the bed, it showed ten o'clock.

My wife turned back the rose-coloured silk eiderdown and placed her dainty feet in bed. She was clad in a thin organdie nightgown through which I could feel her supple and intoxicating form. She looked divine and seductive lying there. Then her pretty feet touched mine. It was glorious. Everything was so beautiful. I could feel her well-shaped legs and knees. We kissed passionately.

The time for which I had been longing for over three years had come. When suddenly I felt a hefty jog and the word 'Chop' rang in my ears. I reeled over and saw the smiling face of Sister McKic. Heaven knows why she was smiling. I certainly wasn't.

TWENTY-FIVE YEARS AGO

In May 1919, Nurse Edith Cavell's body was brought to England and was interred within the precincts of Norwich Cathedral. This heroic woman was shot by the Germans on 12th October 1915. She had been tried for harbouring refugees. 'I am glad to die for my country,' were her last words.

Captain Sir John Alcock and Sir Arthur Whitton Brown, British aviators, crossed the Atlantic for the first time. Leaving Newfoundland at 4.28pm on 14th June 1919, they landed in Ireland at 3.40am 15th

June. The King, in recognition of their great performance, bestowed the honour of knighthood upon them.

FIFTY YEARS AGO

HRH the Duke of Windsor, now Governor of the Bahama Islands, formerly King Edward VIII, was born on 23rd June 1894.

100 YEARS AGO

Sir George Williams, philanthropist, founded the Young Men's Christian Association in 1844. He was knighted in 1894. He died in 1905 at the age of 84.

THE GREATEST SCOURGE

Malaria is one of the greatest scourges that afflicts the human race. It was once common even in the British Isles. It is said that Oliver Cromwell died of it. The old town of Goa in India once boasted a population of 300,000. Then one day Malaria visited the town and then the population dwindled. Today, it has 100 inhabitants.

Malaria is caused by a parasite transmitted by certain mosquitoes. They suck blood from an infected human being, and become themselves infected, their bite in turn, spreading the disease.

Mosquitoes breed in stagnant waters. For years, the most effective cure for Malaria was Quinine, extracted from a bark, which originally came from Peru. It was introduced to European doctors by the Countess of Cinchona. Now, a greater success is said to be the new medical preparation, Mepacrine. Meanwhile, scientists strive for a still more effective preventative for Malaria, one of the worst diseases of mankind.

JOKES...

Have you heard about the Scotsman who learned to read Braille to save light.

Temperance Societies are usually sent to try us.

A modern version of an old saying in these days in England is, 'Cut your coat according to your coupons'.

During the next five months we may expect something over 150 inches of rain to fall. This will surely remind us of an English summer.

THE CHURCH AND SOCIAL ORDER BY PADRE WORSLEY, SENIOR CHAPLAIN

Even suppose we were to change our monetary system and provide state education for all up to 17 years of age - suppose we do abolish slums and build fine cities, improve old age pensions, overcome malnutrition and master unemployment - keep the country strong and give a square deal to the underdog. Suppose we do all this - there is still no guarantee that we people of England will be one wit better or happier unless all this is prompted and accompanied by a spiritual recovery.

The above statement from my address at the service at Tower Hill Barracks on Sunday 19th March drew a request from the Editor of this paper for further elucidation, so here it is.

Let me say, first, that I believe that great changes, after this war, have got to be made, but change for the sake of change (or of appeasing agitation) does not necessarily spell Progress. We want, if possible, to guarantee Progress. The changes, sweeping though they may be, will eventually take place in their stride, so long as our eyes are fixed on the ultimate objective, i.e. Progress.

Speaking very broadly, the social goal of the average Englishman I would be bold enough to say is:-

(a) A sufficiency of the world's goods to be free from want and free from financial worry.

(b) Opportunity to develop his own personality and talents to their capacity.

(c) The right to live in peace and happiness within the confines of his own home, which, itself, should be a dwelling befitting his requirements.

(d) A guarantee that his children have the same opportunity as any other children and that in the event of his death, his wife is provided with a sufficiency as not to have to live in poverty.

If that is the average man's goal, and the church would be the first to maintain that from a social angle, his goal is a legitimate one. Then, I say, let us keep our eyes fixed on the goal and see if we can discover the means to that end.

Thus far, the Christian and the Materialist may (or may not) be in concord. It is at this juncture - the means by which to attain this goal - that they will come into a conflict of opinion.

The Materialist will either say, 'Encourage private enterprise, increase competition, expand exports, develop trade, and so on.' Or he may say, 'Change the economic system, put an end to private enterprise, nationalise land and property and place industry on a more socialistic basis.' The church replies, 'Much of this is excellent, but you have omitted the first essential by which you ensure that when you have attempted much of this by legislation you really reach your goal, and that is a Spiritual Recovery'.

'But Why?' the Materialist asks. 'Because,' replies the Church, 'unless there is a Spiritual Recovery you will be trying to achieve the impossible, i.e. to make a better world without making better people.'

Will you consider this

essential point with me?
What does the Church mean by
Spiritual Recovery? It means
a recovery of the Faith which
so many of our generation seem
to have lost or abandoned.
A sincere belief in God, who
made up all the world, and
in Jesus Christ who redeemed
mankind and demonstrated
the good life. This has
EVERYTHING to do with post
war reconstruction, because if
man will really believe and
act upon that belief, there
springs a basis upon which
to make possible the goal at
which we are aiming.

To put it another
way, there is one of two
possibilities after this war.
The one is the continuation
of the system of excessive
profits, illegitimate gains,
immoral business transactions,
monopolies, industrial
disputes, strikes, lock-
outs, and class antagonism,
all caused by materialistic
selfishness, or greed, or
avarice or love or place and
power, and resulting not in a
better world, but at the very
best, merely in the passing of
a lot of new Legislation, AND
YOU CANNOT MAKE PEOPLE HAPPIER
OR BETTER MERELY BY PASSING
LEGISLATION. The other
possibility (resulting from a
belief that because God is our
Father, therefore, we humans
are brothers of one family,
having a common responsibility
to all) is to put the
interests of the community
before one's own personal
interests. To become in all
sincerity Community Minded.

To accept responsibility
for the common good without
demanding exorbitant rewards.
To work with hand, muscle and
brain, for a common cause
to a Community Plan. To use
one's leisure in the interests
of culture rather than as
an escape from boredom. In
short, to live for an Ideal,
and to develop on a basis of
Christian Citizenship, rather
than in an atmosphere of
selfishness and discord, the
legislative stages, one by
one, which will indeed bring
us to the ultimate social goal
outlined above.

The major fallacy is to
think that the goal can be
reached by short cuts, by
legislation alone, without the
Christian basis.

It is not entirely true
to say that Russia reached
her goal through Communism.
First, she never did reach the
goal at which we are aiming.
Secondly, there is not a
little that is common both to
Christianity and Communism.
(In another sense they are
direct opposites). I believe
that if Russia became more and
more Christian minded and if
Britain became more and more
Community minded, we might
meet and between us not only
ensure the peace of the world,
but fulfil the hopes and
aspirations of millions.

By evolving on sound ethical
foundations that which has
never really existed anywhere
in the world, namely a real
democracy. This would be
progress but it all depends on
'if'.

THE REME DANCE BAND IS OPEN FOR ENGAGEMENTS.

All experienced Musicians.

Write for Particulars: Box 101, c/o The Sierra Leone Bugle, Tower Hill Barracks, Sierra Leone.

NAVY BEAT ARMY

The Army played the Navy at Tower Hill on Saturday, 20th May 1944 in an inter-services match - the first of the season.

Both sides early showed lack of cohesion which one expects at the beginning of the season, though the Navy developed more understanding as the game progressed and at the end were playing well together.

Early play was all in favour of the Navy, and the Army backs and half-backs never got the measure of the opposing forwards.

There was no score at half-time and a switch of Haddow from centre forward, to inside right, Emptage to centre forward from inside left and Hammond from inside right to inside left, brought the promise of better things at the start of the second half which began with the Army attacking strongly. This promise, however, soon petered out, and the Navy returned to almost continuous attack. Their first goal came mid-way during the second half when the Army backs were caught badly out of position. A few minutes later they obtained their second goal following a corner.

For the Army, Haddow was always a trier without getting much support. Jones, of Bandages, also played a strong game at right half but the chief honours on the Army side must go to the goalkeeper, of the CMP who undoubtedly saved the side from a much heavier defeat.

From an Army point of view, the match was very disappointing and the need for more players of class is urgent. The Navy on the other hand, show signs of developing into a useful side.

SIGNALS WIN AGAINST PHILOCTETES

The Signals played Philoctetes at Tower Hill on Sunday, 21st May 1944 and won an exciting game by two goals to one.

Play from the start was very fast and Signals held their own against the star-studded Philoctetes side. Although the heat was great, every player put his utmost into the game and we saw a very even first half which ended with no score.

On the resumption of play, the game was again very even but Philoctetes were the first to open the score, but Signals fought back hard and eventually levelled the scores and went on to score a second grand goal.

OTHER RESULTS

Vehicle Coy 1, Bandages 0

WAASC Juniors 2, REME Juniors 1

ESP 2, WAASC Juniors 1

CMP 1, Vehicle Coy 1.

EDITOR'S FAREWELL

Dear Reader

This is the last issue of this publication which I shall edit. Owing to health reasons, I am relinquishing the editorship of the *Sierra Leone Bugle*.

My Associate Editor, Donald E Palmer and Edward H Wood, have intimated their intention of carrying on a new publication for members of HM Forces in this area.

The work involved in producing the Sierra Leone Bugle is considerable and falls on the hands of a small group of people.

Our primary motive in producing the publication was to provide amusement and news of an exclusive nature whenever possible. In short, to produce a real live paper for members of HM Forces stationed in Sierra Leone.

I trust we have fulfilled our aims during the period of our existence.

I must thank each member of the staff, both past and present, for such excellent work. I wish to thank also the contributors of articles to the paper, and the many people, both civilian and service, who have helped in so many ways to make publication possible. Also, Major

General CG Phillips, DSO, MC, Commander of the Sierra Leone Area, for his permission for the publication of the paper and his co-operation at all times.

Our task has always been difficult, and, as many may not be aware, each member of the staff works in his own time to produce the *Sierra Leone Bugle*.

I bid farewell to our many readers and friends who have been so generous in giving us their support, with the express wish that on some future occasion we may meet again.

Good luck to you all,

Sincerely,

John V West

Editor

Past and Present members of *The Bugle* staff

Editor: John V West

Associate Editors: Don E Palmer (Present), Douglas Hopkins, John Barrie Evans, Frank Coppendale.

Editorial staff: Sid Wade, Stanley R West

Production staff: Jack Eyres, Tom McGibbon, Jack Langton

Circulation: Terry Haydon, Douglas 'Spike' Parsons

The title of this publication, *The Sierra Leone Bugle* is registered and cannot be used by any other person or organization.

The Bullom

THE BULLOM

Vol 1 No.1   Saturday 17 June 1944   Price threepence

INTRODUCING *THE BULLOM*

We present the first issue of the *Bullom* in the hope that it will be a worthy successor to the late *Bugle*. The title of the *Bullom* has been chosen because of its association with the West Coast.

This present edition is but a shade of the one we had planned to produce. The original paper was to be a printed one with a stencilled supplement of second front news. We planned to publish it on 10th June but we delayed it a week to suit the printer. We planned to use blocks for pictures and cartoons and we had all our copy at the printers early in the week - but he let us down, and at the last minute we had to set about the job of producing a stencilled copy before our carefully gathered local news - and world news -

had gone absolutely stale. Here we will have hopes of producing the best printed troops' newspaper that has been seen out here. It is our earnest desire to make this paper of interest to all three services and we shall devote space to news and articles of interest to each service in each issue. We aim to give local appeal and we ask the active co-operation of all our readers in giving us news of activities within units.

We would like to tender our thanks to Major General Phillips, DSO, MC for his kind permission to publish this paper and we also wish to express our real gratitude for the enthusiastic help and guidance given to us so freely by Mr Alan B Mathews, Public Relations Officer, and Mr AG Fraser, which has enabled us to face the task of regularly producing this journal with confidence.

May this paper provide you with entertaining reading and capture your interest - and if it doesn't, write to us and suggest some improvements. It's your paper.

THE BULLOM SECOND FRONT NEWS SUPPLEMENT

With this issue we are printing a special news supplement of day-to-day cables from London and correspondents in France. Since our attack on the Fortress of Europe the wireless news has been followed with great interest, but we offer this as a more permanent record of history's mightiest invasion.

NEWS PAGE - DELAYED 'D' DAY DAWNS - COMBINED ATTACK ON HITLER'S ATLANTIC WALL

At 0102 hours on 'D' Day - Tuesday 6th June 1944 - paratroops landed in France to open our attack on Hitler's Fortress. Their immediate task was to silence two coastal batteries which would have caused havoc among our shipping which was to follow them. Seaborne landings commenced at 0600 hours, from 4,000 ships and thousands of smaller craft. Warships bombarded the coast with shells of four to six inch calibre from more than 640 guns. Minesweepers

cleared and kept open the sea lanes. The landings were made mainly on the Normandy coast from the south of the Seine to the Cherbourg peninsular. The whole operation had been postponed 24 hours on account of rough seas. Eleven thousand front-line aircraft were available to provide air cover and these flew 13,000 sorties and dropped 10,000 tons of bombs - over 5,000 of which were dropped on 10 enemy battery positions. By 1000 hours, bulldozers were at work making runways for allied aircraft - behind Hitler's Atlantic Wall.

General Montgomery is in command of American, British and Canadian troops.

6th June: Mr. Churchill announced in the House of Commons our invasion of France. Landing operations continued throughout the day. Airborne landings were resumed in the evening. Direct enemy fire onto the beaches was not neutralised until mid-day. Heavy air attacks on railway junctions - those at Amiena, Serqueux and Chateau Dun in particular.

7th June: Continued progress. 114 German aircraft destroyed. Paratroop landings, including NT and anti-tank guns. Bayeux captured and allies cut the railway from Caen to Bayeux. Sea landings interrupted by weather but resumed later. Air Force flew 9,000 sorties. Further support by Warships.

8th June: Enemy troops near Caen and railway junctions near Paris bombed. Our armour extending a bulge in enemy lines near Bayeux. German radio credit us with six to eight divisions landed. 51 enemy aircraft destroyed. RAF bombed rail junctions at Saumur, Rennes, Fogeres, Alencon and Mayenne. Naval gun fire dealt with enemy batteries firing into landing area from north of Havre.

9th June: Small port of Isigny, 15 miles west of Bayeux, captured by US troops. Continuous front from Isigny to Bayeux. Disembarkation continues although weather still not favourable. Air attacks on railways and, during the night, on airfields at Fleres, Rennes, Laval and Le Mans, from which enemy had supplied most of air support for his troops. Weekend: Bridgehead 51 miles wide which continues contact between Allied troops. British troops reached Tilly. Americans have crossed flooded areas in Aure Valley and high ground near Carentan captured. One Fighter Group established in France. General Montgomery has set up his HQ in France.

12th June: Supreme Allied HQ reports that initial phase of securing Bridgehead is almost over. American tanks have broken into Carentan. Heavy armoured fighting – more intense around Tilly. Enemy counter-attacks at Caen beaten back by British 6th Airborne Division.

RUSSIAN VOLUNTEERS ON INVASION COAST

The German paper says that a considerable number of Russian volunteer units, including Cossacks, Armenians, Turkestans and other Russian units besides the Georgian Legion, are among German anti-invasion divisions on the French coast.

During 1943, 233,000 German soldiers attended Romanian cinemas.

LEAFLETS OVER THE REICH: 'NURSERY TRIPS' FOR FINAL TRAINING

BY WING-COMMANDER LV FRASER

Here for the first time is given an account of Britain's Royal Air Force leaflet raiders – of how Bomber Command week by week, since the war began, has been bombing the enemy and enemy-occupied territory with countless tons of truth-telling literature.

Actually the story goes back even further than 3rd September, 1939, for on 10th October 1914, the first pamphlet-dropping raid was carried out by No.4 Squadron of the then Royal Flying Corps, and in April 1917, the world's first serial newspaper was dropped over occupied Belgium.

This contained the hectic warning – 'The whole world from China to the United

States arms itself against barbarous enemy civilisation.' First leaflets of the World War II repeated that warning. 'Our resources and those of our allies in men, arms and supplies are immense. We are too strong to break by blows and we could wear you down inexorably.' On the night of 1st/2nd October 1939, Berlin received its first bundles of British leaflets. Thereafter stern punishment was meted out to any German discovered reading them. Today RAF leaflet raids on Occupied Europe are carried out by Operational Training Unit crews as a final stage of their training. Known as 'nursery trips' they serve a double purpose.

Exactly the same procedure is carried through from the initial briefing and routing to the target to the interrogation after the return to base, as if the bomber crews were carrying a load of live bombs to Germany. Leaflets must be dropped with precision and accuracy, and with allowance for winds which might scatter them over the countryside instead of in towns. Regular supplies of pamphlets are delivered by the RAF to Germany, France, Holland, Belgium, Norway, Denmark, Italy, Czechoslovakia, Luxembourg, Hungary, Romania and Bulgaria. Nor are the Channel Islands forgotten. Leaflets are also dropped profusely in Far Eastern campaigns.

To France, the RAF delivers two weekly newspapers, Le Courrier de L'Air and Revue de la France Libre. The latter consists of exacts from leading articles in the London and Provincial press with cartoons from British morning and evening newspapers. A recent issue of a four-page British Courrier de L'Air published photographs showing the remains of the Messerschmitt works at Augsburg after the great Allied attacks on 25th February and 13th April. In addition to the two weeklies, two monthly tabloid magazines - La Revue du Monde Libre (48 pages) and Accord (32 pages - illustrated) are delivered by the RAF to the French people.

Germany receives weekly newspapers - the RAF *Luftpost* and monthly revue Dio Andere Seite. Week by week, in pictures and news paragraphs, they reveal to German people the full extent of the destruction done to Nazi industries by Allied bombings. They disclose too that the U-boat fleets under the command of Admiral Dönitz are only sinking one out of every 1,000 ships sailing in convoy. Dio Andere Seite - 'the other side' - provides further food for German thought. One of their own great writers, Thomas Mann, pours loathing and contempt on the Nazi movement. Letters from German prisoners of war tell of the good food and treatment they receive. As the war approaches its climax, so the volume of aerial propaganda is being stepped up. In July 1943, 10,914,550 leaflets were dropped over Europe by the RAF. Half that number were dropped over the Reich. In March 1944, 55,982,541 leaflets (including newspapers booklets and magazines) were dropped, of which nearly 23,000,000 fell on Germany. Since the outbreak of the war the RAF have dropped 1,264,456,656 leaflets on Europe. They are dropping them now at the rate of 1,200 per minute.

ANOTHER SUCCESS

In presenting *Youth at the Helm* at Tower Hill Theatre on Thursday 8th June, the New England Repertory Company gave a fine performance which was appreciatively received by a large audience. Hubert Griffith has written and produced a remarkably fine comedy which has not a dull moment and which provides many bursts of spontaneous laughter. The story tells how Randolph Warrender insinuates himself on the staff of a London bank and, by a colossal piece of bluff, brings into being a vast industrial project, winning for himself in the process both the Managing Directorship of the enterprise and the hand of the heroine.

That may sound impossible to anybody who did not see Ronald Jones' excellent

interpretation of the author's ideas in his characterisation of the completely self-confident bounder, Randolph Warrender. His confident acting convinced us that it could have happened. Not one of the company over-acted their part and the whole show was most enjoyable. We hope we shall have the pleasure of seeing this able company again - and soon, too.

GERMAN CONFERENCE ON MANPOWER AND MORALE LANDSMEN FOR REPLACEMENTSBY AJ MCWHINNIE

Landsmen to stiffen the German Navy's morale may go to the immobile surface warships to release seamen for U-boats. Berlin fears the rot of idleness. Men of the German SA - sound party men - are being called on to serve with the German Navy and Mercantile Marine.

A secret navy conference has been held at Stettin. The German Navy had several Admirals there to hear Wilhelm Schepmann, Chief of Staff for the SA, promising his organisation would help to ease naval and merchant navy manpower problems. Schepmann is a landsman leader of landsmen.

In a spirited speech he scoffed at Britain's sea power - to the discomfort of Admirals whose plans had been wrecked by the very sea power which this SA leader tried to belittle. Then Wilhelm Schepmann wound up by saying:

'The SA will regard it as its paramount task to provide men for the Navy and Mercantile Marine. Submarine men need long training.'

At first glance it might be assumed these SA men are needed particularly to replace the large number of submarine men who have perished in the many U-boats which have been sunk during the last year, but before men can man a submarine they need fundamental training. They need the most specialised skill for undersea service. It seems much more likely that these SA men earmarked for the Germany Navy will be drafted to Hitler's idle surface ships for basic training in seamanship while others will be called to the German freighter service.

This would have a double advantage. Firstly, men who already have general sea experience will be released by SA for underwater training in U-boats and, secondly, storm troopers will be specially instructed to do all they can to stiffen morale in the ships to which they are allotted.

SHIPS THAT NEVER SAIL

In Berlin they cannot forget that the first signs of revolt in 1918 started in the idle service ships. While there is no reliance placed in London or Washington on history repeating itself, German Naval and Mercantile chiefs are not convinced that it cannot happen again.

Men stationed on board fighting ships which never come out to fight must be affected by the news that their people living under the shadow war plants and military targets are also living under the shadow of death by bombing. Yet they and their men folk are doomed to spend months, even years in fine ships which never steam out on the high seas. It is hoped that the newcomers will bolster their morale and those seamen whose morale is good and who are ready for battle could thus be given an opportunity to fight in U-boats.

For at least six of the last twelve months more German U-boats have been destroyed than Allied freighters have been sunk by U-boats. This suicidal rate of U-boat expenditure means a loss by death or capture of something like 50 trained and skilled submarine men with each U-boat which is destroyed. Somehow these men must be replaced. Reserves of submarine crews have dropped to a dangerous level. Dönitz never believed ways would be found of sinking so many of his U-boats. He thought in 1939 his reserve pool of personnel arrangements was more than adequate.

DOOMED UNDERSEA SAILORS

Now that they are proved hopelessly inadequate he looks round for sources of replenishment and men in his idle surface ships - having at least training and experience of the sea - offer the best material. He will rush them through a course of submarine training ready to take their places in the U-boats now coming off the stocks to replace those he has lost during the last few months.

But Dönitz knows - and the men of the U-boat army now know - that the average life of a U-boat in 1944 is only about a quarter of the time it takes to build a U-boat.

Expectation of survival for present day German U-boat men is therefore lower than expectation of life in any of the world's fighting forces.

SPECIAL *BULLOM* REPORT:
NEW TOWER HILL CHURCH DEDICATED
GOVERNOR PRESENT AT OPENING CEREMONY

The Right Reverend JLC Horstead, MA - The Lord Bishop of Sierra Leone - at a most impressive service dedicated a new church at Tower Hill Barracks on Whit Sunday, 28th May 1944 in the presence of His Excellency the Governor Sir Hubert Stevenson KCMG, CBE, MC, who was attended by Mr. Peter Wilkins, ADC and personal secretary. Others present included Vice Admiral AM Peters, CN and Mrs. Peters; Colonel FV Oborne (representing Major General Phillips, DSO, MC), Sir CA Jardine, CB, DSO, MC; Colonel the Viscount Downe, Lieutenant Colonel FL Fowden, TD; Mrs. Horstead, the Reverend RL Palmer, a distinguished African Minister who acted as Bishop's Chaplain, and many officers and men of local units, together with a representative body of civilians.

The First Lesson was read by Colonel Oborne and the second by the Reverend W Farrer, DACG, WA.

In his address, Bishop Horstead said that in his many contacts with troops serving in this area he found they were broadly divisible into two groups - those who were disappointed that there were so few of the pleasures and entertainments here they were used to at home, and those who were indignant that the Colony had seemingly advanced so little under British rule. The Bishop then pointed out that about ten years ago this Colony had celebrated the Centenary of another feeling of indignation - an indignation which had culminated in the abolition of slavery. At this Centenary a stamp was issued which showed a picture of a young slave boy shackled to the ground by chains. The chain was carried around the border of the stamp and there it was broken - broken by a cross. The presence of the cross is significant. This significance explains the existence of this Garrison Church. The cross breaks more chains than that of slavery and without religion life is denied most of its meaning.

Music for the service was provided by Captain HS Denton, MA, ARCO, piano; Mrs May, violin and Captain Wright, flute - a trio of musicians whose spirited leading of the singing and beautiful voluntaries were much appreciated. Major GW Wellington, tenor, was the soloist. The Bishop's procession was led by Sergeant L Vokes, carrying the Cross, followed by the Server, Corporal JB Evans. Staff Sergeant J Enderby was Sideman.

The Church is to be the centre in which many week-night activities will take place. It is due to the thoughtful planning of the Reverend GS Worsley, and, though primarily designed as a Church, it will also be used with due regard for the sacredness of the building, for lectures, concerts, plays and discussions. Possibly in the future our Churches will be used more for these things; at least this is a fair and carefully planned experiment.

BEST CONCERT FOR MANY YEARS

A concert, described by one Old Coaster as the best for many years was held in the Garrison Church on 31st May. A well varied programme was enthusiastically received by a large audience.

F/O Maynard (Organist of Bath Abbey) in his first group gave a fine interpretation of the Bach Prelude and Fugue

and his playing of Fantasie-Impromptu was distinguished for its subtle variations in touch and tone control. We were indeed fortunate to have the services of two such fine singers as Father Mackey and Sergeant Cunnah. The last named has a wide experience of concert work and his rendering of *Hear Me, Ye Winds and Waves* was possibly the finest feature of the programme. Although short of practice, he showed fine range, well produced tone and splendid breath control.

The two trios showed an effective ensemble. The individual solos of Mrs May and Captain Wright were distinguished for their good intonation and tone quality.

The concert was admirably organised by Captain HS Denton who played the piano part of the trios and accompanied the singers with fine understanding. Great praise is due to him for his untiring efforts to organise a concert of such quality and yet retain that popular appeal which modern music goers are supposed to require.

COLONIAL DEPENDENCE ON HOME SUPPORT

The short-sighted parochial-ism of the British electorate in the past to Parliamentary Legislation on the grand scale - particularly where finan-cial grants and subsidies were involved - may be understood, but cannot be sufficiently deplored. Nothing could be more valuable to induce a new view of the integral relation existing between the Mother Country and its dominions and dependencies and addresses similar to that given by Mr AB Mathews, Public Relations Officer Freetown, in the Tower Hill Garrison Church on 1st June.

Such informed officials as Mr. Mathews should be engaged to impress on the minds of the many who are seeing temporary service in the Colonies that it is at once the duty and the interest of the home-staying Briton to assert constructively that economic and social inter-dependence which must link the members of the Empire if it is to survive.

It was apparent from the questions which followed that Mr Mathews had thoroughly stimulated his audience, but he had to assume in them a deeper understanding of Colonial administration than many of them had, owing to the scope of his thesis and the brief time at his disposal. How very worthwhile it would be if he, or some of his staff, could spare the time to lead half a dozen discussions, spread over as many weeks, to cover the same ground in greater detail, with attention given to more particular aspects of Colonial administration with which the temporary resident here is naturally unfamiliar. The interest undoubtedly exists.

THE SIEGE OF TOBRUK

A most interesting lecture on The Siege of Tobruk was given by Major GW Welling from first-hand experience in that historic event, in the Garrison Church on 7th June before a good audience.

His survey of the period of the siege was very comprehensive and his account gave us the satisfaction of knowing that those oft unsung heroes, British Troops, once more withstood all the hardships and difficulties and shouldered their job unrelieved for the whole duration of the siege in their customary brilliant manner. After all the propaganda other Allied troops have received, it was a welcome tonic to hear such a generous tribute to our own comrades.

We hope in our next issue to be able to give a special article by Major Wellington on his personal experiences in Tobruk.

LATEST NEWS CABLES FROM LONDON

The latest news cables we are able to include before going to press are those dated 15th June. Commenting on the 19th Communiqué from Supreme HQ Allied Forces, they say the highlight is the advance in the Sablons-Baupte region. Several miles west of our troops is some high ground which dominates communications along the west side of the Cherbourg peninsular. If we

could reach this high ground,
we might effectively cut off
the peninsular. Thus London
commentators expect the Germans to react fiercely to our
latest advance.

ITALY

Yesterday's advance was one
of the biggest we have made
lately. It now looks as
though the Germans may next
try to stand on a line from
Piombino to Lake Trasimeno,
thence to Perugia and
Spoleto. Each day in Italy
there is increasing evidence
of the disintegration of the
German 14th Army commanded by
General Mackensen. It seems
there is little left of it
beyond scattered remnants
who are mainly engaged
in stealing one another's
transport to get away as
quickly as possible. Some
stragglers who have been
captured bore official passes
authorising them 'to proceed
either alone or in small
groups to the assembly area
near Florence'. The 14th
Army consisted originally of
the 4th Parachute Division,
65th and 362nd Infantry
Divisions and the 3rd Panzer
Grenadier Division. The 715th
Infantry Division was totally
destroyed before the present
disorganised withdrawal
started. Kesselring has now
thrown into battle every
division he had in Italy
except the single Deport
Division employed in the
North on Security duties.

He has also drawn in one
division from Denmark -
the 20th Luftwaffe Field
Division.

SPECIAL WAR CABLE: LEAP-FROGGING THE PACIFIC, RESTORING THE BALANCE IN BURMA

Events during the past week
have given the Japanese, as
well as their European Axis
partners, cause for much
disquieting reflection.

The Burma Campaign
clearly has not been going
according to the Japs' fond
expectations. Following
their failure to bring off
a sensational coup at Arakan
and the reverses they have
suffered there, their much
boosted offensive at Manipur
has been effectively checked
and with the advent of the
Monsoon seems likely to peter
out with heavy casualties.

Now Allied operations
in the north of Burma have
suddenly presented the Japs
with extremely awkward and
unpleasant complications that
had certainly not entered into
their calculations.

UNITED NATIONS ATTACK

With this grave new turn for
the Japs, fortunes in Burma
have seen further ominous
happenings in the Pacific
- another Westward leap-
frogging Allied attack on
Dutch New Guinea mainland and
Wakoe Island in its vicinity
and air attack by aircraft
of the Mountbatten, Macarthur

and Nimitz Commands upon the Japanese port of Surabaya.

This latter is a significant indication of the close co-ordination of the Allied effort from the Indian Ocean to the Pacific and must have a most uncomfortable morale for the Japs for shadowing as it does the shape of things to come. As British, American, Australian, French and Dutch airman participated in this attack, which did considerable damage to Jap shipping, oil refineries, docks and airfields, it was very much a United Nations effort.

AGONY COLUMN

A Yank sergeant was spending his leave in London. He had viewed the splendour of St Paul's and Westminster Abbey, when turning to his guide, he said, 'And now I want to see the Church of England'.

The latest schoolboy howler in answer to the question 'State what you understand by the term "separate peace" brought the reply "Divorce"'.

Have you heard of the chorus girl who was so hard that only diamonds made any impression on her?

Recently overheard in the YMCA: 'I saw a grand handbag down the road'. 'How much was it?' 'I don't know I hadn't any brandy with me.' 'Darling you have a figure like Dorothy Lamour,' said the ardent lover. 'Well, let's not go over that again,' said the girl.

Husband: 'How long have those two been married?' Wife: 'Not long. They've been here a week, and I haven't heard either of them slam a door once.'

'Have you much room in your new flat?' 'Gracious no! My kitchen and dining room are so small I have to live on condensed milk, dehydrated fruit, and shortbread.'

SPORT
RAF BEAT ARMY
RESULT: RAF 3, ARMY 2

The Army met the RAF in the second representative match of the season at Tower Hill on Saturday 3rd June. From the start, play was fast with the ball travelling quickly from end to end. The RAF generally swung the ball about better than the Army and their combination was always slightly better. There was no score at half time. The second half started in storming fashion with play again even and it was not until half way through this period that the scoring started, Borrowman opening for the RAF and later adding a second. Andrews scored for the Army from a penalty and Edwards scored the best goal of the match. The RAF retaliated and Mather scored the winning goal just on full time.

RED CROSS GAME
RESULT: ENGLAND AND WALES 3, SCOTLAND AND IRELAND 1

His Excellency The Governor was present at Tower Hill on Saturday 10th June 1944 when England and Wales played Scotland and Ireland. Collections at half time and proceeds from the sale of programmes were in aid of the Red Cross Fund.

A big crowd watched a thrilling game with England and Wales generally that little better. Two fine first half goals for England and Wales came from Perry and Tredway.

Scotland and Ireland started the second half in grand style and soon reduced the lead with a good goal by Haddow, but England and Wales later scored a further goal through Tredway from a free kick.

EDITORIAL NOTE

The Bullom is produced from Tower Hill Barracks under the joint editorship of Sergeant D Palmer and Sergeant EH Wood, who will always welcome articles on items of local news for publication. Readers' Letters are also invited and we hope to publish an interesting selection in each edition. Address all correspondence to: The Editors, *The Bullom*, c/o Camp Commandant, Tower Hill Barracks. The willing help of Sergeant E Carmichael who drew our title page heading and whose work will be seen to advantage in a printed edition later, and Corporal T McGibbon and Lieutenant Corporal J Ayes (production staff) and Lieutenant Corporal T Haydon (distribution manager) is also gratefully acknowledged.

COMING HOME

Home seemed never to be far from the soldiers' thoughts, never better expressed than in a poem, written by one of Sid's army buddies:

I feel,
When blossoms blaze with every vivid hue,
And whispering waves reflect the sky's deep blue,
Unreal.
It seems as though these things should never be,
For beauty now is meaningless to me.
I am not stirred, I have no eyes to see.
I know,
Hibiscus flowers that glow the deepest red,
And palms that tower in splendour overhead,
But oh,
They are not real, they're empty hollow things,
A mirage, or a vivid dream that clings,
To waking hours, and vague disquiet brings.
But soon, I know that there will be a happier day.
I'll gaze with joy at skies of sombre grey.
A boon, To feel the cutting sting of wind-blown rain,
And all this beauty that I now disdain,
I'll feel once more, I shall be home again.

In Sid's letters, too, lurking beneath the surface of the trivial chit-chat there was a barely suppressed longing to go home. One letter, written in early 1945, said little or nothing about his life in Africa and was far more preoccupied with thoughts of home:

Dear Mum and Dad.

With the exception of a brief note at Christmas time, this is my first letter for nearly a month. I apologise for this, but believe me that it is all I can manage to get letters to family written, which I have to squeeze into odd moments.

I was pleased to receive a message from Dad, the first I believe he has written. However, I know he always joins you in all the good wishes expressed in your letters.

I was most annoyed to read how your house, bombed last summer, is still in such a leaky and inconvenient condition. How you manage to live all day in artificial light without going dotty I don't know, and the slackness of repairing it, if no good reason can be given, is a very poor show. I hope that this will soon be rectified. I am looking forward to about four and a half months' time when, with a load of luck I shall be looking out for a boat which will bring me home again.

I am pleased you received your Christmas card on time and that you liked it. It was ready months before Christmas, but I kept it until someone was going home so that you could have it on Christmas Day.

We enjoyed a very fine Christmas and celebrated the New Year with equal gusto. The next celebration I partake in will be the best of the lot, and that should take place as soon as I see the distant outline of England.

In spite of the inconvenience of your home, I notice Granddad is still doing well. Please give him my best wishes. I should like to see him out here. He would have the time of his life walking up and down the veranda, but he would not see many people to talk to.

I suppose you are still getting cold weather in England, and I hope it is all gone before I come home. If the temperature drops to 70 degrees Fahrenheit, I feel as cold as ice and lately have started wearing thick shirts on these occasions. Goodness knows how I would stand the climate in England if suddenly transferred. Before coming home in the winter, the fellows usually spend a time in a temperate climate where they get used to the weather. But being as I hope to be home in the summer, this should be unnecessary and perhaps I should get straight home.

When home, I shall have to wear all my special thick clothing and carry on taking medicines which are supplied before we leave here. Actually, it is as risky a business to come home to England as it is to come out here, but I have been very fortunate. Surprisingly enough, my feet have been better here than ever before, and all my corns have been rotted away. I have two foot baths per day, so they should be OK.

The only thing I am frightened of when coming home is seeing a Yorkshire pudding or a meat pie again – the shock will upset me – but not for long.

Cheerio, with all my love…

Entries in the Leave pages of Sid's Army Pay Book tell the story of his
time away: 22nd October 1943, two weeks leave, then nothing more
until an entry for 28 days leave beginning on 16th March 1945.

Sid Wade, the reluctant soldier, didn't have to wait until summer to come home. He
returned to England and took 28 days leave, starting 16th March 1945, in time for his 31st
birthday on 24th March. A few weeks after his return his wife was rudely awoken early
one morning by a loud thumping noise and opened her eyes to find her husband bashing
his boots as hard as he could on the bedroom floor. When asked what he was doing, he
explained he was banging the spiders and scorpions out. And this in deepest Essex.

It was the slightly surreal things like this that were to stay with Sid for the rest of his
life, long after he had forgotten – or perhaps forced himself to forget – the harsh climate,
horrible diseases, hard work, exhausting route marches and the never recounted rare
times of true danger he had encountered in Africa. The bad times were rarely mentioned
after his return, only the strange or humorous incidents were retained.

Nine months after his return, on Christmas Day 1945, his first and only son was born.
It doesn't take a mathematical genius to work out how I, the author of this book, came
into existence, the true epitome of a post-war boom baby!

So I grew up, listening to my father's stories of his time in Africa, the good times and the humour, but rarely anything about the misery which I'm sure he endured in equal, if not greater, measure.

Returning to civilian life, he worked for a while as a salesman before returning to the print trade to work for the Roneo company in Essex. In his spare time, in a shed at the bottom of his garden, he ran a small printing business, which eventually expanded and allowed him to work for himself full-time as a jobbing printer and later as proprietor of a stationery shop in his home town of Barking. In 1972 he retired to the Essex coast, where, for a few years, he ran a sweet shop in Harwich, before giving up work completely and moving to Dovercourt.

But, even though Sid kept many things to himself, it's clear that aspects of his African experience, good and bad, stayed with him. Even years after he returned, when he thought no one was listening, he could often be heard humming to himself what would have been one of those old songs from the NAAFI as, to the tune of *The Mountains of Mourne*, he could be heard quietly singing:

> *Oh I shall be happy, wherever I roam,*
> *When I'm ten thousand miles from Sierra Leone.*

ACKNOWLEDGEMENTS

A major part of this book lies in the appeal of its pictures, some of which were taken by the soldiers with amateur cameras, but a great many more of which originated in professional postcards and souvenir photographs, bought in West Africa during the 1940s. The only clue to who owned the copyright on these professional images was in the wording printed on the back of each postcard, which read: *Copyright Reserved. Lisk-Carew Brothers, Real Photo Card, Freetown, Sierra Leone. Patronised by HRH The Duke of Connaught.* A convoluted trail to find the copyright holder took me from Africa, to the UK, onwards to Canada and finally to America. Along the way, my thanks go to:

Rachel Rowe, Librarian for South Asian and Commonwealth Studies at the University of Cambridge Library in the UK, who remembered a Canadian student who had previously enquired after Lisk-Carew copyright details. Rachel's records led me to…

Julie Crooks, who lived in Toronto of Sierra Leonean parentage and who, at the time I was writing this book, was completing a dissertation on early photography in Sierra Leone and specifically the work of the Lisk-Carew family. Julie helpfully made an introduction for me to…

Ronald Andrew Lisk-Carew, JP, MBA, DSW, CQSW in Birmingham, USA, who, after checking with members of his family, kindly gave permission to use the pictures.

Posthumous thanks must also go to the many now unknown soldiers who, each in his own way, contributed to the book, and especially of course to Corporal Sid Wade, reluctant soldier, artist, photographer, scrap book keeper and father, without whom this book would never have been started, let alone finished.